Buying and Selling Your Home

David Lewis is the Executive Editor of 'Money Mail', the *Daily Mail*'s personal financial section which is published every Wednesday. He has been writing on matters relating to home ownership and personal finance for many years, having previously been editor of the monthly magazine *Money Management* and before that worked at the Consumers' Association on *Money Which?* magazine.

Over the years David Lewis has written many articles, advocating the consumer point of view in the field of home ownership and insurance. In 1977 this was recognised by the Government who appointed him for a three-year term as consumer representative on the newly formed Insurance Brokers' Registration Council.

TEACH YOURSELF BOOKS

BUYING AND SELLING YOUR HOME

David Lewis

TEACH YOURSELF BOOKS
Hodder and Stoughton

First printed 1980
Second impression 1981

British Library C.I.P.

Lewis, D
    Buying and selling your home. – (Teach yourself books).
    1. House buying – Great Britain – Handbooks,
    manuals, etc.
    2. House selling – Great Britain – Handbooks,
    manuals, etc.
    I. Title   II. Series
    333.3'37   HD1379

    ISBN 0–340–25114–X

Printed and bound in Great Britain for Hodder and Stoughton paperbacks, a division of Hodder and Stoughton Ltd, Mill Road, Dunton Green, Sevenoaks, Kent, (Editorial Office; 47 Bedford Square, London, WC1B 3DP) by Richard Clay (The Chaucer Press), Ltd., Bungay, Suffolk

Contents

Preface   viii
Acknowledgements   ix

1 **Why own a Home?**   1
   As an investment; Changing home; The costs of buying
   versus renting.

2 **Finding Somewhere to Buy**   8
   Where to buy; House prices; When to buy; What type of
   house or flat; Old, modern or brand new; National House-
   Building Council; Freehold or leasehold; Mobile homes
   and caravans; Houseboats; What to look for; Making an
   offer; Gazumping; Surveyors and hazards.

3 **Buying Your Council House or Flat**   32
   People who have done it; Reselling; The right to buy;
   Mortgages and options; Shared ownership; Homesteading.

4 **Initial Costs**   39
   Deposit; Solicitors' charges; Land registry fees; Stamp
   duty; Inspection and survey fees; Removal, decorations,
   furniture.

5 **Finding a Mortgage**   45
   Advance planning; Choosing a building society; Homeloan
   scheme; How much they will lend you; Do not overstretch

yourself; How much they will lend on the property; Disliked property; Additional security; Mortgage not big enough; Interest rates; Other lenders: local authorities, insurance companies, banks, employers; Speeding things up; Mortgage brokers; Bridging loans.

6 **Repaying a Mortgage** 61
Repayment mortgages: full, option, low start, high start; Mortgage protection policies; Endowment mortgages: full with-profits, lower cost, non-profit; Which type of mortgage for you; Why mortgage illustrations may mislead; Ending your mortgage early.

7 **Conveyancing and Solicitors** 73
The legal process; Other things that solicitors do; Choosing a solicitor; Doing your own conveyancing; Cut price conveyancing organisations; Scotland; Northern Ireland; Forms of ownership.

8 **Household Insurance** 88
Buildings insurance; How much to insure for; Contents insurance; New-for-old; Legal liability; Legal expenses insurance.

9 **Living in Your Home** 97
Rates and rateable value; Water, gas, electricity, fuel, telephone; Other bills; Service charges; Heating; Maintaining your home; Noise; Disputes with neighbours; Securing your home.

10 **Thinking Ahead** 109
Improving or extending your home; Renovation grants; Holidays; Second homes; Falling on hard times: divorced, widowed or separated, elderly people; Taking in lodgers.

11 **Moving Out** 117
Estate agents; Auctions; Selling your home without an agent; Showing people round your home; Furniture removers.

12 **Your Home and Tax** 123
Tax relief on mortgage interest; Dependent relatives; How to get tax relief; Capital gains tax; Capital transfer tax.

13 **How to Save Money** 130

Appendix 1 Alternatives to buying   133
Appendix 2 Mortgage Repayment Tables   143
Appendix 3 Useful Addresses   150

Index   161

Preface

This book is for first time buyers and sellers: for people, who are in the process of buying a house or flat for the first time, who are thinking of doing so in the future, or who already own their first home but have not yet experienced selling a home as well as buying one at the same time.

Every effort has been made to make this book accurate. However neither the publishers nor I can be held liable for any incorrect information. The book includes details of the 1981 Budget as well as the Housing Act 1980. The right to buy for Council tenants came into effect on 3 October 1980. And the other provisions of this Act are now fully effective. So when I refer to 'will have' in this context, the reader should read 'has'. Certain details may have changed since the book went to press and I have indicated where this is likely in the text. The list of names and addresses in the Appendix should enable you to get a second opinion on any point which is particularly important to you or which may have changed.

If readers have any experiences which might be of interest to me regarding future editions, I would be happy to hear from them; write to me care of the publishers. However I am unable to give personal advice.

David Lewis, March 1981

Acknowledgements

My thanks to those who read the draft of this book. They include three English solicitors and one Scottish: all of them made many helpful suggestions and to my surprise and delight actually liked the contents. In addition my colleague Janice Allen kindly read through the draft.

I am indebted to Ernest Testa, an estate agent and surveyor (who read Chapters 2, 9, 10 and 11); Geoffrey Randall of the Shelter Housing Advisory Centre (Chapters 1, 10 and Appendix 1); the 'backroom boys' at the Woolwich Equitable Building Society (Chapters 4 and 5); the Corporation of Mortgage, Finance and Life Assurance Brokers (Chapter 5); Steven Haberman, Lecturer in Actuarial Science at the City University (Chapter 6); the British Insurance Association (Chapter 8); and Jack Morgan, consultant to the Income Tax Payers Society (Chapter 12); and Alan Cooklin, Principal Lecturer, College of Law, Chancery Lane (Appendix 1).

Also my thanks to the organisations which supplied information and the permission to reproduce tabular material, the source of which is given with each table.

Last but not least, thanks to my wife Susan who helped with the research, thoroughly edited my first draft and made innumerable helpful suggestions.

1

Why own a Home?

An Englishman's home is his castle – or so the saying goes. And what better way of ensuring the security of that castle than by owning it. Every year a higher and higher proportion of houses and flats become owner-occupied, either bought outright, or with the help of a mortgage. And each year nearly 400,000 homes are bought by first time buyers.

Over half of the twenty-one million homes in the UK are owner-occupied; the rest of the population live mainly in rented accommodation, either from local authorities (34%) or from private owners (9%). Other sources such as homes tied to a job (3%) and housing associations (1%) account for a very small proportion.[1]

So if you want to buy your own home you are in good company. Over two-thirds of the respondents to a survey [2] gave owner-occupation as their ideal in two years' time, while only 52% were already owner-occupiers. At younger ages the survey showed that the desire to become an owner-occupier was much stronger: nearly one in two respondents aged under forty-five who currently rented ideally wanted to become owner-occupiers within two years.

These figures are hardly surprising. Owning your own home has many obvious advantages over renting, even assuming you can find somewhere to rent. One of the intangible reasons is that you feel you have freedom to do as you want. You are independent. And people seem to be happier with their lot when they own rather than rent. You can choose where to live and usually when and how to decorate.

On the other hand the cost of repairs and maintenance, and the necessity to organise these yourself, is seen as one of the few disadvantages of owner-occupation. Another is the heavy financial burden which people have to take on when they buy a home for the first time. Mortgage arrears, after rent arrears, are the most common reason for homelessness.

As an investment

The most important reason for owning your home is that you are making an investment which, in terms of value for money, most people will find impossible to repeat. Owning a home is such a good investment because house prices have tended to keep pace with, and often exceed, the rate of inflation in the economy as a whole. This does not mean they always will – or that you can never lose money by owning your home. But if the past is any guide to the future, inflation is likely to continue at current rates and house prices are likely to go up by as much or more. Owner-occupied homes are also exempt from capital gains tax when you dispose of them (for exceptions see p. 127).

You might wonder why rises in house prices are such an advantage. After all if you do not own one already, the rise in prices may appear sickening. But once you own your home, and stay in it for a few years, you will soon see how price rises can work to your advantage.

Table 1 shows the average price of dwellings bought by first time buyers through building societies since 1969 together with their average mortgage and average income. Take the couple who bought in 1969. Suppose their mortgage was exactly the average at that time – £3,240. Their mortgage interest rate was then $8\frac{1}{2}\%$ and their payments came to, say, £26.38 a month. At the beginning of 1980 the mortgage interest rate was a much higher 15%, which means their payments would have risen to £41.77 a month.

Table 1 First time buyers

Year	Average price £	Average advance £	Average income £
1969	4 097	3 240	1 617
1970	4 330	3 464	1 766
1971	4 838	3 914	1 996
1972	6 085	4 954	2 281
1973	7 908	6 115	2 734
1974	9 037	6 568	3 231
1975	9 549	7 292	3 753
1976	10 181	8 073	4 285
1977	10 857	8 515	4 800
1978	12 023	9 602	5 283
1979	14 918	11 286	6 290

Source: The Building Societies Association and Department of the Environment: 5% sample survey of building society mortgage completions.

However average incomes, in spite of incomes policies, have over the same period gone up by much more as you can see from the table. So while their repayments have not even doubled, their income has meanwhile probably almost quadrupled from £1617 to £6,290. Thus the mortgage payments are far less onerous to our couple than for those just starting on their first purchase. If the same couple were first time buyers of the same house in 1979, they would have to find the payments on the average mortgage of £11,286 (£145.49 a month) out of their earnings of £6,290 a year. Alternatively they would need to provide a much larger deposit than was needed only ten years ago.

Changing home

Of course most people do not stay in the same home all their lives. In another survey[3] of 16,000 borrowers with mortgages from the Alliance Building Society, the results show that the average stay in the present home is just under five years with a peak stay of from two to four years.[4] The longest stay in a current house was sixty-six years. But 20% said they expected to move house within two years and another 20% in two to five years' time. However some people expect to stay put for a long time. 27% expected to stay in their present homes indefinitely – and another 5% for ever.

Why do people move home? The Housing Research Unit casts light on this too. Desire for more space was given as a reason by 43%; a better location was wanted by 38%; because of their job said 26%; more privacy was wanted by 25%; financial reasons influenced 23%; and 20% wanted a larger garden.

Apart from 36% whose reason was to buy a home of their own (first-time buyers), other less common reasons were to escape some environmental nuisance (16%), getting married (14%) or related to schooling (8%). A tiny proportion moved house in order to accommodate an elderly relative, wanted less space in the home or a smaller garden.

So you are unlikely to be content to sit back for long in your castle and reflect on how lucky you are to have such a small mortgage now in relation to what today's first time buyers are having to cope with. You will go in search of a better home for whatever reason and probably not far from where you already live – most people move less than ten miles from where they were before and according to the Nationwide Building Society survey,[4] 51% move less than five miles. You will not be able to get a larger mortgage than a first time buyer if he earns the same as you. But what you will have is the increased value of your present house to invest in the new one.

Table 2 shows the same information as Table 1 but this time it applies to former owner-occupiers, that is, people who already own their home, and who are buying a new one with a mortgage.

You can be pretty sure that in most cases these people are increasing their mortgage when they move.

The table shows that whilst former owner-occupiers obtain slightly higher advances, on account of their slightly higher incomes, the value of the home they are buying is much greater

Table 2   Former owner-occupiers

Year	Average price £	Average advance £	Average income £
1969	5 148	3 460	1 987
1970	5 838	3 854	2 168
1971	6 666	4 407	2 466
1972	8 965	5 538	2 748
1973	11 900	6 273	3 118
1974	13 049	6 577	3 618
1975	13 813	7 409	4 299
1976	15 160	8 509	4 997
1977	16 246	9 101	5 558
1978	18 792	10 611	6 161
1979	24 074	11 837	7 101

Source : The Building Societies Association and Department of the Environment: 5% sample survey of building society mortgage completions.

than the value of those bought by first time buyers. While they are paying much the same for their mortgages, their earlier home ownership allows them to enjoy larger and more luxurious homes at little extra cost because of the substantial deposits they are able to provide.

The costs of buying versus renting

The greatest difference between buying and renting is that when you buy you have to find a large lump sum of money at the outset. Mortgages mean that you can pay off a lump sum by instalments over many years – but it is rare that you will get a mortgage for 100% of the purchase price except from a local authority, where it is quite common. So even with a large mortgage you need a deposit. Then there is also the cost of legal expenses, possible repairs and decorations, new fixtures and fittings which, if you rent, often do not apply or may be provided by the landlord.

However private landlords often charge one month's rent in advance and may require a deposit in advance of another month's rent – and there may be a flat agency charge to pay as well. You may also be expected to pay for 'fixtures and fittings'. The cost of these fixtures and fittings is often inflated in spite of the fact that it is usually against the law for a landlord to grant, or a tenant to transfer, a residential tenancy in exchange for extra money. None of these costs normally apply to Council tenancies.

Comparing averages can be misleading. According to a Government report:[5] 'There is no incontrovertible way of making the comparison [on subsidies] between home owners and local authority tenants to show the extent of the advantage of one group over the other or even to show which group "does better".'

With privately owned housing the subsidy (tax relief) is more concentrated – it is given to those with the largest mortgages who pay the largest amount of interest. Contrary to popular belief these are not necessarily the rich but are more likely to be first time buyers who have little capital of their own to put up. Council tenants pay the same rent as their neighbours however long they have been tenants – although rent rebates (and rent allowances for private tenants) can lower the cost for the less well off. Nowadays most first time buyers are newly married couples who have spent a short time in rented accommodation or seek to buy their first home even before they get married. The statistics are quite clear in their message: the sooner you get on the home ownership ladder, at however modest a level, the more likely you will be able to eventually own the house of your dreams.[6]

NOTES

1 *General Household Survey 1978*, Preliminary Results, OPCS Monitor, May 1979.
2 *BMRB Housing Consumer Survey for the National Economic Development Office*, HMSO, 1977.
3 *Housing Research Unit*, University of Surrey, 1977. Similar results were found by the *General Household Survey 1977*, HMSO, 1979.
4 Nationwide Building Society, *Home Owners on the Move Survey*, June 1979.
5 *Housing Policy Technical Review*, Chapter 5, HMSO, 1977.
6 *Social Trends 1980*, HMSO, p. 205.

2

Finding Somewhere to Buy

Most people who advise on house purchase start by asking how much you can afford and then proceed to see what kind of house or flat suits your pocket rather than your needs. I think you should first try and sort out in your mind what kind of home would suit you best and if after a long search you cannot afford it, then you can settle for the nearest which you can afford, sacrificing some features which you rate as less important.

Where to buy

The main criterion for choosing a house or flat is that it should be a sensible distance from your place of work. If you and your partner both work – and your jobs are in different directions – your scope for choice of location is going to be limited to somewhere between the two jobs or else one of you is likely to end up changing your job before long.

If you work in central London you might choose to commute quite long distances by rail; but remember rail services do vary and a sixty mile journey which might only take an hour on one route could take two and a half on a less popular line. Check the cost of a season ticket to your place of work from your newly chosen home and whether your employer would give you an interest free season ticket loan. In other locations you are more likely to travel by bus, so check on the service's frequency and convenience.

Most people also like to live near relatives and people they know. If this is important to you, you will have limited considerably the area of your search. In a city, for instance, you often find people divide into north of the river and south of the river people. Rarely do they think of crossing to the other side in search of a home; they prefer to stick to the area they know.

Other points about the general location of your new home will assume different levels of importance depending on your circumstances. For instance if you have children of school age, the availability and quality of local schools and their distance from your home will be of prime consideration. In fact some people move home in order to get their children into the catchment area of good state schools. If you do this you should make quite sure that your children will get into the school of your choice – and that your new home is in the catchment area. I have never heard of such a case but I presume that catchment areas can change – and it would be unfortunate if someone moved house in search of better education for their children only to find they are not much better off than they were before.

Local transport, as opposed to commuting, is also worth thinking about, especially in rural areas where public transport can sometimes be very sparse. If you cannot get to the railway station without a car, then your wife is either going to be an unpaid chauffeuse twice daily or she will need a second car; according to figures put out regularly by the AA, the cost of running a car seems to run a close second to the cost of owning a home. A decision to run two cars should not be taken lightly. Perhaps this is the time to ask for a company car?

Availability of shops is also important. In the country, if you have a car, it is easy to drive to the nearest village or town. But the larger the town, the greater becomes the proliferation of yellow lines, parking restrictions and traffic jams and it is often more convenient to walk to the shops. So unless the nearest shop is less than a quarter of an hour's walk away, you are likely to want to take the car or a convenient bus.

Whether to live in the town or in the country is a decision which seems to perplex some people. I live in town and I know people who live in the country; we seem to be equally happy. But that may be because I live in an area of town where there is a lot of open space. Parks and trees and squares add to the quality of life and you can be sure that such amenities will reflect in the price of the home you are seeking.

House prices

A host of factors influence the price of a house. The most obvious effect of this is the range of price you can pay for indentical houses situated in different parts of the country. Not only do the prices for similar houses vary nationally but they rise and (less commonly) fall at differing rates.

Table 3 illustrates this. The first column is a regional index of house prices with the national average price as its base. With an index rather than the actual prices, it is easier to see just how prices vary in different parts of the country. For example, if you buy in Greater London you can expect to pay £128 for every £100 people on average over the whole country are paying. But in Yorkshire and Humberside you would only pay an average £77 for the same sort of housing.

You can see that if you move from the Outer Metropolitan Region to the East Midlands you are going to get a much bigger and better house for your money. But if you move the other way, as people tend to want to do, what you get for your money is going to be a lot less desirable.

The second column of Table 3 shows how prices have increased during one year. Far from the differences between the areas being reduced with the passage of time, it seems house price rises, at least at the time of the survey, were highest in places which already showed the highest prices. There are sometimes special regional explanations for sudden house price increases. In Scotland the exploitation of North Sea Oil has had a tremendous impact on the price of housing in areas adjacent to the oil industry. And parts of London have seen prices rocket as Middle Eastern magnates have moved in looking for a home from home and little caring for the cost so long as they liked it.

Table 3   Index of average house prices by region

	Index	Increase in region over 12 months %
United Kingdom	100	+29
Greater London	128	+34
Outer Metropolitan	133	+27
Outer South-East	112	+35
South-West	103	+34
East Anglia	96	+36
East Midlands	77	+27
West Midlands	93	+25
Yorks & Humberside	77	+27
North-West	85	+28
Northern	78	+23
Wales	87	+33
Scotland	99	+21 to +27
Northern Ireland	104	+16

Source : Nationwide Building Society Housing Trends, fourth quarter 1979. Index calculated from prices in the survey.

When to buy

There is a popular season for house buying and selling. It starts in January but most activity seems to take place in the spring with April as the peak month. I suspect the actual amount of buying and selling activity depends much on the local weather. With a particularly mild winter, it probably gets started sooner; with a sharp cold spell with snow at the end of March, people probably give up for a while. It can be quite depressing tramping around from one expensive unsuitable house to another – and if it is pouring with rain or you are chilled by a bitter wind, you are more than likely to want to pack up and go to the cinema instead.

On the other hand for a buyer, if you can bear it, bad weather is just the right time to be house hunting. It will show the house at its worst – and if you like it then, you will certainly love it when the sun is shining. What is more, particularly if prices are rising, other house hunters are likely to be after the same property as you are. But you will be on the spot – while your possible competitors are at the cinema. You must hope that the seller thinks nobody else is interested – not that they have merely been put off by the bad weather.

A shorter season occurs in September. There is not much activity in July or August when most people go on holiday, nor in November or December presumably because it gets dark very early and people are immersed in Christmas festivities. But if you happen to be looking at such times, you are more likely to pick up a bargain. People selling in November or July, for example, usually have some special reason to do so, rather than wait for for the traditional seasons. They may be moving home to take up a new job in another part of the country or a previous offer may have fallen through for reasons entirely unconnected with the house. They may be getting divorced or want the money urgently. Or they may just have been asking too much during the season and nobody made them an offer. Do not hesitate to ask why someone is intending to move especially if you think there is some reason connected with the house – perhaps they hated every minute they spent in it! Most likely their answer will be much more down to earth.

What type of house or flat

What type of house you buy is usually determined by what you can afford and the space you need. Most people look for something which has a minimum of a sitting room, kitchen, bathroom, and indoor wc, and two bedrooms – one for themselves and one for guests or children. In addition many people will probably

want three or four bedrooms in total, a dining or second reception room, a downstairs toilet, and possibly a study or breakfast
room. These seemingly basic requirements can disguise enormous
variations in size. It is therefore unwise to set your own particular needs too rigidly. Remember some three bedroom houses can
be larger than four bedroom ones – and you should think hard
as to how much you will actually use that tiny guest room. Perhaps a larger bedroom for each of the children might be more
useful.

Homes come in all shapes and sizes; they are usually classified
as detached, semi-detached, terraced, bungalow, purpose-built
flat or maisonette, converted flat or maisonette. The availability
of each type of accommodation varies between different parts of
the country. Table 4 shows where different types of property
are likely to be found. Flats are more likely to be found in Greater
London – terraced houses in the North and Midlands.

Detached houses

When you first think of a home of your own you probably think
of a large house situated in the middle of its own spendid garden.
You may picture it as brand new or as a sixteenth-century manor
house and you will be pleased to know that there are such detached
houses of all ages throughout the country. The main virtue of a
detached house is that it is detached. You can usually walk all
the way round it. You do not share any walls with neighbours so
you will not be disturbed by noise coming through the walls; nor
will you cause such a disturbance yourself. Detached houses
tend to be larger than other types of houses with the same
number of rooms. They are also likely to have larger gardens.
Other factors such as age, design and size are also likely to be
important to you.

Semi-detached houses

Semi-detached conjures up a vision of suburbia; and a great
many semi-detached houses will turn out to be very similar in
appearance, style and size. They were mostly built between
1919 and 1939 and were sold then for as little as £500 each.
The typical layout is kitchen, sitting room and dining room

downstairs; two reasonably sized and one tiny bedroom, with a bathroom and separate wc, upstairs. There are also larger four bedroomed versions which have a breakfast room and some may have a downstairs toilet. Semis built since then are likely to be

Table 4   Regional variation of types of houses

Region	Dwellings as % of total in each region				
	Detached	Semi-detached	Terraced	Purpose-built flat	Converted flat and other
Great Britain	16	33	28	15	8
Greater London	6	20	25	26	23
South-East	24	33	25	10	8
South-West	22	34	25	9	10
East Anglia	30	36	22	7	5
East Midlands	24	39	26	6	4
West Midlands	12	41	30	12	5
Yorks & Humber	14	42	31	8	5
North-West	9	37	36	11	6
Northern	8	42	35	11	4
Wales	19	35	34	5	7
Scotland	13	18	20	40	9

Source : The General Household Survey 1976, HMSO 1978.
Crown Copyright

similar in layout. However those built during the period 1939 to 1959 may be less attractive than older ones, often having smaller dimensions and a different finish – plain red brick compared with the attractive pebble-dash popular in the thirties. Few people set out to live in a 'semi'. A great many end up in one.

Terraced houses

Terraced houses are increasingly popular with first time buyers. Most are in towns and they tend to be relatively cheap compared with other houses. They also can be very small: a typical terrace may originally have had 'two up and two down'. Nowadays you can expect to buy them with an added back extension comprising a kitchen and bathroom. Sometimes the rooms upstairs have been reorganised to make three tiny bedrooms – or the two reception rooms knocked into one to create more space.

The main drawback to a terraced house is the lack of space – once a couple start having children they soon grow out of their terraced home; until then they are likely to be very happy with it. According to the Alliance Building Society[1] the highest failure rate in obtaining mortgages on the type of house of the purchaser's choice included those looking for terraced houses and those wanting wings of large houses; this may be caused by a certain resistance to old property amongst building societies and the fact that terraced houses usually predominate in run-down inner city areas where building societies may prefer not to lend. But the high proportion of first time buyers who do buy terraced houses with the help of a building society mortgage shows their popularity.

Bungalows

Bungalows are generally in demand from elderly people – and also from the disabled. The reason is obvious. They do not want to climb stairs but like to retain their own garden. About one in ten building society mortgages are given on bungalows; they are less likely to be found in large towns because, room for room, they use up a lot more ground space which if in short supply makes them more costly.

Purpose-built flats

Purpose-built flats are blocks of flats which were originally built as flats. They are mostly on long leases and you pay a small ground rent, say, £50 a year; you also have to pay your share of the cost of maintenance and services (e.g. porter, lifts, outside decorations and repairs) and the charges of the managing agents who keep the place running. These charges rise annually as costs rise. Older people who do not want to be bothered with the responsibilities of organising maintenance themselves prefer purpose-built flats. Generally a residents' association is formed and there is nearly always someone willing to take up issues with the managing agents on behalf of all the tenants. Similar considerations apply to the so-called 'mansion' or refurbished blocks of flats. The only difference is that the cost of maintenance is likely to be higher when expensive items like roofs, lifts and communal heating need to be repaired or replaced.

Residents' associations are not without their problems. Often they tend to be organised by one or two 'public spirited' individuals who, as a result of the apathy of the other residents, may represent their own taste or views as that of all the residents to the landlord. The result may be changes made in your name of which you do not approve.

Converted flats

Converted flats are mainly found in London although they do exist elsewhere. They are often large Victorian family houses which are large enough to contain a good sized two bedroom flat on each of three floors and a basement; some houses are large enough to contain two small flats or one large one on each floor. Sometimes an extra flat is added in the roof space. The obligations with a converted flat are similar to a purpose-built one.

Converted flats may be difficult to obtain mortgages on, however – see p. 50. The main difference between a converted flat and a purpose-built one is that the landlord, who only gets a small ground rent, is not likely to be interested in acting as unpaid managing agent. And, there being so few tenants, they need a unanimous decision before they can put pressure on the landlord.

A typical complaint is that the landlord does not clean the common staircase adequately. Often it is better for the tenants to agree to arrange this sort of thing themselves rather than pay for services arranged by the landlord or agent which they are not satisfied with. These converted flats often have gardens – sometimes the use is shared by all the flats, sometimes it is exclusive to the resident of the basement or 'garden' flat – and sometimes it is even cordoned off into a zone for each resident. If you want a garden to yourself make quite sure that you have it. I know of a case where someone bought a garden flat thinking he had sole use of the garden; he entirely replanted it at his own expense only to find the other residents turning up with their deckchairs on the first hot summer day and they had every right to do so.

Maisonettes

Maisonettes are like mini-blocks of flats. They often look like semi-detached or terraced houses – but there is a separate dwelling upstairs and downstairs. Sometimes the term maisonette is used to describe a flat occupying two floors. However the main difference from a flat is that you usually have your own front door on to the street.

Old, modern or brand new

Whether you want an old or modern house is a matter of taste. So long as the house has been well maintained then there will be little difference between the prices of older and more modern houses which offer the same accommodation and facilities. The standard of houses built today is said to be a considerable improvement on those built fifteen years ago.

Brand new houses

You can of course buy a plot of land and get a builder to build the house of your dreams to your own design. But most new houses are speculatively built by builders and property developers whose business is building houses for sale.

With a new house you can buy from the plan – that is put down a deposit to reserve your house even before it is built. You can expect the price to rise between the time you do this and the time you complete the transaction. You would be wise to inspect a show house – that is a similar house to your own which is finished and put on show – before you commit yourself. Rooms can look deceptively large on a plan. Remember also that builders invariably choose the best house or flat as a show house – and others on the same estate may be less attractively situated.

New houses have the disadvantage of having to be run-in.[2] The garden is often not made up – and you may have to buy top soil to cover rubble left behind after the building. You will almost certainly have trouble with condensation; a typical newly built house contains 1,500 gallons of water which have to be dried out.[3] There can be other teething problems, too, such as delays in the completion of the house and your having to move in before tiles on the kitchen floor have been laid – an example one person told me about.

National House-Building Council

There are often minor and sometimes major defects to be put right on new houses. The National House-Building Council, with which all the large firms of developers and builders and many smaller ones are registered, offers an important protection to purchasers of new houses. The Council has laid down minimum standards of workmanship, material and design – and the Council is supposed to ensure that during the first two years from purchase, the builder puts right at his own expense any defect resulting from his failure to comply with these standards. However you must complain to the builder in writing within the time limit.

In the third to tenth years the protection is limited to major structural defects not covered elsewhere. The worth of this cover was brought home to some residents on an estate near Colchester where a large number of houses started to collapse as a result of having been built on a former rubbish dump. To safeguard against inflation up to 15% a year you may have to pay an extra once and for all premium when you buy the house; this is strongly recommended.[4]

Freehold or leasehold

With a freehold you have no landlord, you pay no ground rent, usually you are beholden to no one else – and you own the house for ever. With a leasehold you have a landlord to whom you must pay ground rent for a certain number of years until the lease runs out. Most leases run for ninety-nine years. However under the Leasehold Reform Act 1967 you often have the right to buy the freehold or get a fifty year extension to the lease of your house (but not of a flat).[5] The differences can become blurred because you may have to pay a rent charge or chief rent on freehold property in some parts of England[6] or *feu duty* in Scotland.[7]

Houses or flats with leases granted for twenty-one years or less have no rights to have their leases extended unless the lease contains an option to do so. You are unlikely to get anyone to lend you money on such short leases as, by the time you have repaid them, the lease will be nearly expired, and your asset will no longer be a worthwhile security.

Covenants

Leases usually contain a number of covenants which bar the resident from doing such things as letting any part of the premises (except, perhaps, the garage), using the premises for business purposes, displaying any sign (including a For Sale notice), erecting any building or structure, changing the fences, keeping pets, singing or playing a musical instrument or gramophone after 11 pm, or even putting up a television aerial.

However freehold houses can also have covenants (called 'restrictive covenants') just like those listed above – and on housing estates these have been known to include forbidding the running of a mobile fish and chip shop from the home or car breaking in the garden! More irritating are those preventing your changing the colour of your front door without permission of a residents' association or determining that you should hang net curtains in the windows.

Often the restrictions are ignored, especially if the person who might want to enforce them (like the ground landlord of a lease) is not around. But with freeholds there is no landlord, so policing of the covenants is only significant on housing estates where it is often in the hands of the residents' association – possibly run by neighbours who care rather strongly if you move in and start painting what was always a grey front door – red.

Mobile homes and caravans

Caravans, often referred to as mobile homes, have one great disadvantage. Most people who own them do not own the 'pitch' on which they stand. Under the Mobile Homes Act, 1975 they have the right, with a few exceptions, to get a written five year agreement – with an option to extend for a further three years. But unless they buy the land on which the mobile home stands they have no security after this. And even when they buy the plot they will be moved off if planning permission has not been obtained for the mobile home. This is a problem often encountered by gypsies who wish to settle in one place while their children go to school.

Some mobile homes are more akin to 'prefabs' than caravans. The distinguishing feature from ordinary homes is that they are not attached to the ground – generally they are placed on a concrete bed on the site. And due to the fact that they are not intended to be moved, they cannot easily be towed away to another site if the rent for the site increases beyond that which the tenant can afford, or the landlord wants a large premium to grant a long lease.

By their very method of construction even the highest quality mobile homes have a much shorter life than conventional housing, seldom more than twenty to thirty years, while a conventional house might last one hundred or more. They tend to be small and the materials used may make the mobile home a fire hazard. As a deteriorating asset they cannot be bought with a mortgage although the purchaser may be able to obtain credit from a bank or finance company. Maintenance, however, is less costly and complex than with a conventional home which may make them attractive to elderly people.

A Government report[8] concluded that the main advantage of a mobile home is its cheapness and they are really only worth considering for people who cannot afford to buy a conventional home, either because their incomes are too low or they cannot save a big enough deposit. A second-hand unit bought on a site with a five year lease might be a viable alternative to private renting while waiting for council accommodation. More details of the rules can be found in an official leaflet.[9]

Houseboats

Houseboats are a similar case to mobile homes. Unless you own the mooring you will have to sail off somewhere else if the rent gets to be more than you can afford. Like some mobile homes, many houseboats are not designed to be moved easily so this may involve you in some expense. Unlike mobile homes, they are also likely to need quite a lot of maintenance – painting more regularly than a house and making sure that no leaks spring up. I have known only one person who lived on a houseboat. She went out one night to the pub with her husband – and they returned to find their home had sunk!

What to look for

By now you may be itching to get started in your search for your new home. Finding out about available property is pretty straightforward. Get in touch with all the estate agents in the area where you want to live. Tell them the sort of thing you want and ask them to send you details of anything suitable which they get in. In Scotland most property is sold through Solicitors' Property Centres.[10]

It is worth calling in at an estate agent's office – if only because you are more likely to get better service that way. The fact that you take the trouble to call shows him you are serious. If a building society has indicated its willingness in principle to lend to you, make sure the agent knows. If you already have finance fixed up you are a much better prospect to him. If you are moving to an area a long way from where you live at present, make use of the service of Home Relocation or the National Network of Estate Agents to put you in touch with a local estate agent.

Do not just rely on agents sending you information. Drive or walk round the area looking for 'For Sale' boards. Some may be 'under offer' but it is often worth a telephone call to find out. Also look for advertisements in local and national newspapers. This is where to find the homes of people who are selling without an agent. It is also worth asking any local people you know whether neighbours are thinking of moving. Even a short visit to the local pub might be more rewarding than you think.

There are a number of weekly magazines which specialise in house advertisements such as *Dalton's Weekly* and the *London Weekly Advertiser*. There are also monthly magazines such as *House Buyer*, *Buying Your Home* and *Home Finder* which are useful if you are looking for a new house on an estate. So go down to your newsagent and buy all they have got – you probably will not need more than one copy of each of the monthly magazines as the advertisements tend to be from the same builders. If there does not seem much property available you might consider inserting a 'Property Wanted' advert in a local newspaper.

Never agree to pay an estate agent commission to find you a house – it is the seller who employs an estate agent and it is he who should pay him. If you write to an agent just ask for details of available property of the type you want – do not let him think you have commissioned him to find a house for you (for which he might insist on charging you).

Get yourself a map of the area before you start viewing – it will save you a lot of wasted time. Sometimes estate agents give them away free. Remember that it is an estate agent's job to make every house or flat seem as attractive as possible. The checklist opposite will help remind you of your needs – an estate agent will not tell you what the house lacks when you fall in love with the split level reception room and spiral staircase.

Checklist for house hunters

Number of bedrooms
Bathroom
Separate wc
Fitted kitchen, space for washing machine, drier, etc.
Size of sitting room
Separate dining room
Second bath and/or wc
Extra room, e.g. study, workroom, guest room
Garage, car port, parking space and parking for visitors
Garden, patio, terrace, balcony, space for greenhouse or garden shed
Space for alteration or additions
Cupboards and storage space, warm linen cupboard
Central heating and hot water
Extras included, e.g. carpets, curtains, light fittings, fridge, cooker, TV aerial, etc.
Convenience for public transport and shops

Before you step inside

Many is the time you will know that a house is not for you even before you have pressed the front door bell. Do not sneak away – sellers get used to people who are not particularly interested and it is worth getting an idea of what is on offer and at what price.

You may even be able to save yourself a journey. First of all pinpoint the house on your map. Is it convenient for the bus route or close (but not too close) to the railway station? Is it too close to any likely sources of noise, e.g. school, pub, dance hall, main road, railway line, airport, police, fire or ambulance station, hospital with a casualty department, workshop or car repair yard; or to any unpleasant smell, e.g. farm, factory or stables. With both noise and smell the direction of the prevailing wind is important; if six out of seven days a week the smell or noise is blown in the opposite direction it will not be such an inconvenience.

Does the house have a garage, car port or space for off street parking where you might build a garage later? Are the reception rooms of the house south facing? If they are north facing it will be a cold dark place to live in. And is the garden likely to get much sun? Remember the sun is much lower in winter than in summer, but if there are trees nearby they will look much smaller without leaves – and in summer, though decorative, will allow a lot less light through. Nearby buildings also cut off light – especially in the winter when the sun is low. They may also intrude on your privacy: can the garden or rooms in the house be seen into easily by passers-by or neighbours?

Once you are inside

Having pressed the door bell, you are then welcomed in. As you are shown round the house look out for the points mentioned in the estate agent's blurb and do not be afraid to ask if something is not mentioned.

First impressions can often be good indications. Remember the seller will have done his best to make the house as attractive as he can – you should be seeing it at its best. Is your immediate impression that it is poky, characterless or cold? If it is the odds are you will not want to buy it. On the other hand property can look quite different at different times of day. If your first appointment is on a winter's afternoon or evening, make sure you go back and take a look when there is more natural light.

Even if your first impression is bad, it might not be anything a fresh coat of paint would not cure. As you go through, envisage where you would put your furniture. Will everything fit in? Where will the television set go? Is there a broom cupboard and enough kitchen cupboards and surfaces? Are the rooms a workable and usable shape? Is it possible to get to the dustbin from the kitchen without walking through the main living room? Has the room you are likely to be in most got a pleasant view? Does this room have direct access to the garden? If you have plans for kids, would you be able to see them at play in the garden from the kitchen? Is there room for the kitchen appliances you have or might buy in the future? Would you have to keep the washing machine, dryer or freezer in the garage? If so is there plumbing and electricity already laid on there? Is there central heating and does the boiler also heat the hot water? If applicable where is the fuel stored? What are the fuel bills? What are the rates?

Are the carpets and curtains included? (Do not ask unless you want them.) Are light fittings and for that matter anything screwed to the wall or ceiling included? Ask specifically for any item you want and make a list of those that are included or agreed as extras. Also make a note whether the plumbing or electrical system is antiquated; if there are lead or iron pipes or round pin sockets you are likely to be in for a pretty hefty plumbers' or electricians' bill in due course.

Always go into every room – even on to a balcony. It may seem much bigger than it really is. Is there room for a pram in the hall – if you need it? Is there anywhere to hang coats? Will your car fit into the garage with enough room to open the car door and get in and out? Has the house been well looked after? Has it been newly decorated – often a sign of cracked walls beneath? Are there signs of damp or bad condensation? If enough things build up to put you off now, it is much better than getting cold feet about the deal after you have paid the cost of a surveyor and solicitor.

Ask why the sellers are moving? If they are similar to you in age and outlook and have been happy but outgrown their home, then the odds are you will be happy too. If they appear to resent your reasonable questions, it may be because they have something to hide.

Ask about the neighbours: what do they do and how old are they? Young and old can mix very well but this is not always the case. If possible go and have a chat with them. They may tell you about any likely snags, e.g. all the houses in the area are subsiding or they have been campaigning to prevent a major road being built in the vicinity.

Making an offer (Except Scotland)[11]

When you find a house you like do not be afraid to ask the people who are showing you round if you can talk privately for a minute or two with your partner to find out what you each think about it.

If you want to make an offer to buy, show both enthusiasm and reticence: enthusiasm to show that you are really serious and want to buy; reticence because you do not want the price to be raised – and perhaps you can even get it down a bit. A figure to aim for is 5% off. But play it by ear: do not hesitate to make an offer there and then if you really like the place. You cannot be held to anything you say verbally – a property contract must be in writing.

If you do make an offer and it is accepted, make sure you give the seller your name, address and both daytime and evening telephone numbers. Give him the same details about your solicitor. Get the seller's full name, address and telephone number (day and evening) if you do not already have this information. And get details of his solicitor. In the case of solicitors, give and obtain the name of the person who will actually be dealing with the transaction.

Then write to the seller confirming your offer and his acceptance but *make quite sure* that you include the words 'subject to contract' either immediately after your offer or at the top of the page. By doing this you can withdraw later without obligation. You can also add 'subject to survey' if you wish. And you might want to send a copy to the seller's estate agent to discourage him from sending more people to look round.

Specify everything which the seller has agreed to include in the sale – curtains, carpets, fitted cupboards, light fittings, television aerial. Some sellers have an unfortunate habit of asking for more money for such extras if it is not made clear from the start what is included. Ring up your solicitor and send him a similar letter telling him the name and address of the seller and his solicitor. This will start the legal process described in Chapter 7.

At this stage the estate agent may ask for a deposit. This is not necessary and your best tactics are to refer him to your solicitor. If he insists on a deposit before the contract is signed, make sure he is reputable, i.e. he belongs to one of the recognised estate agents' organisations or tell him you will pay it to the seller's solicitor. In either case you should send a letter with the deposit stating that it has been paid to a 'Stakeholder subject to contract'. If either side withdraws later before contracts have been ex-exchanged, you are entitled to a full refund.

At a sale by auction a spoken offer is binding if accepted by the auctioneer. Once the auctioneer's hammer has fallen to the highest bid, he is authorised to make a binding contract on your behalf and you must pay him a 10% deposit. So you need to find out all about the house, have it surveyed and so on, before the auction takes place. If you subsequently withdraw, you lose your deposit.

Gazumping

Having stressed the importance of making your initial offer 'subject to contract' so that you can withdraw later without obligation, it should not surprise you that the seller can do the same. At times when prices are rising and there is a lot of demand for property, a 'sellers' market' may develop and the seller may receive other offers almost as soon as he has received yours. If you have offered him less than the asking price, it would seem reasonable that he accepts yours subject to someone else coming along and offering him his advertised price. Unless the seller instructs him not to do so, an agent is under a legal obligation to pass on all offers he receives until contracts have been exchanged.

Gazumping describes the situation where you have made an offer, usually at the full asking price, but later the seller decides that he wants more money from you. This may be because he has had another higher offer from someone else or he may just think you are very keen and might be prepared to pay him more. The gazumper usually gives the impression that he is going to sell to you but then shortly before contracts are exchanged and after you have incurred legal, survey and other expenses, he insists you pay a few hundred or even a few thousand pounds more. If you do not agree, he says he will sell to someone else.

Gazumping became a common phrase in England in 1972 when the practice of raising the asking price after a 'subject to contract' offer had been accepted became epidemic in some parts of the country. The expression gazumping is used in the United States to describe the sharp practices of second-hand car dealers.

However when demand for property declines and mortgages are in very short supply, gazumping quickly fades away. And then it may occasionally be replaced by the reverse practice of a buyer pushing the price down when a seller is desperate to be rid of a slowly moving property.

Surveyors and hazards

When you are buying a house or flat, you should always instruct a surveyor and get a written report. This may be quite costly but he should be able to tell you quite a lot about your new home which you would not necessarily notice yourself.[12] The building society 'inspection' is not a full structural survey – and is not a lot of use unless the building society refuses to lend on the property. If the house seems in bad condition you might hold back on your own survey – there is not much point in finding out what is wrong if the building society is not interested. From 1981 major building societies are sending copies of their inspection report to buyers; previously you could not see them.

Choosing a surveyor

Your best bet is to get a personal recommendation from someone you know who has used a surveyor in the same area. Local knowledge can be important in surveying; for example areas affected by mining subsidence will be well known locally but might be missed by an outsider.

There are surveyors in independent practice and these might be worth trying in preference to those tied up with an estate agency. Surveyors with the letters ARICS or FRICS after their name are members of the Royal Institution of Chartered Surveyors – but there are surveyors who belong to other estate agency and valuation bodies including the Incorporated Society of Valuers and Auctioneers – see Appendix 3.

It is best to get a list of three or four names and ring round and discuss your requirements. They will want to know the approximate size of the house and where it is and should be able to give you a quote there and then. Once you know their fees, choose the one you judge is likely to do the best job if there is not too much difference in what they charge. When you commission the surveyor ask for a 'full structural survey'. There is no point in him supplying measurements of rooms – so it is worth telling him you do not want them.

If you are buying a flat or maisonette, instruct the surveyor to assess the state of the whole building as well as your flat. The flat may be fine – but if the roof or foundations are rotten there could be an extremely high maintenance charge on its way. You might be able to save money if the building society surveyor agrees to do a full stuctural survey at the same time as he does his inspection for the society. Check also that your surveyor has an errors and omissions insurance policy to cover him if he misses something and you have to sue him.

Interpreting a survey report

Some survey reports are likely to disappoint but do not be too disheartened. In 1970 *Which?* magazine commissioned six different surveyors to survey the same house in London. These surveyors spent from one and a quarter to nine hours on the job, wrote 1,000 to 4,100 words in their reports, charged from £31 to £95 and valued the house from £9,000 to £11,000.

There were also some surprising discrepancies between the different surveyors' reports.

Which? reported:

'*Surveyor E:* All external walls have recently been repointed and painted.

Surveyor B: The main rear wall ... requires complete re-pointing above ground floor level.

Surveyor C : Some pointing is required mainly at low level to the brickwork.

Surveyor A : Generally, the pointing of the brickwork is in good condition.'

A similar exercise in Devon with four surveyors did not show up quite so badly and I still think a survey is worthwhile especially for a first time buyer.

Do not be put off by a pessimistic report. Provided the building society is still prepared to lend, a bad survey report is a means of knocking the price down – or getting the seller to do repairs before he leaves. Always remember the seller is usually as anxious to sell as you are to buy.

If a surveyor does not follow your instructions, for example, you ask him specifically to inspect the foundations and he does not, do not pay him in full – or make him go back and finish the job.

The surveyor's report should advise you of any additional tests he considers necessary, e.g. rot, woodworm, wiring or drains. But there are a large number of reputable woodworm and rising damp and dry rot specialists who do inspections and provide written reports free of charge.[13] If the house is old it is worth having one of these as an added protection; again try and get someone to recommend a firm they have used and been pleased with. You have to pay extra for an electrician or for a builder to test the drains.

NOTES

1   *Housing Research Unit*, University of Surrey, 1978.
2   For further advice get the booklet *Your New House* published by the National House-Building Council.
3   For further advice get *Condensation*, Advisory Leaflet No. 61, Department of Environment/PSA, HMSO.
4   Get the free leaflets *Safeguards for Buyers of Newly Built Houses* and *The Ten Year Structural Protection*, National House-Building Council.

5 See free leaflet *Leasehold Reform*, Department of Environment, Welsh Office.

6 You can buy them out under the Rent Charges Act, 1977. See free leaflets *Rent Charges*, *Apportionment of Rent*, Rent Charges Act, 1977; *Calculation of Redemption Prices*, Department of Environment.

7 *Feu duty* in Scotland is an annual payment similar to a ground rent. No new *feu duties* can be created, and existing *feu duties* must be redeemed by the vendor on a sale. See Tenure Reform (Scotland) Act, 1974.

8 *Report of the Mobile Homes Review*, Department of Environment, HMSO, 1977.

9 *Mobile Homes: A Guide to the Rights of Residents of Caravans and other Mobile Homes*, Department of Environment.

10 For addresses see free leaflet *Buying or Selling a House?*, Law Society of Scotland.

11 This section on making an offer does not apply to Scotland – for what to do there see the appropriate part of Chapter 7.

12 For how to attempt to do your own survey: Ball, R. and Pittaway, A., *The Whole House Omnibus*, Fontana/Collins 1979; see also reports in *Which?* and *Handyman Which?*, May 1979.

13 For example members of the British Wood Preserving Association, British Chemical Dampcourses Association.

3

Buying Your Council House or Flat

If you live in a council house or flat, is it worthwhile buying the home you live in – if you get the chance? In the past whether you have been able to buy your council house has depended on the politics of your local authority; some Conservative ones were quite willing to sell off houses to tenants; most Labour ones were not. Council flats were rarely sold at all.

But the situation is now changing and under the provisions of the 1980 Housing Act[1] most council tenants from 3 October 1980 will be given the right to buy the house or flat they live in. Most important of all will be the right to buy the home at a discount ranging from 33% to 50%[2] depending on the length of time the tenant has spent as a council tenant. It is this discount which makes buying a council house or flat especially attractive.

People who have done it

Since 1970 some councils have been selling their property to tenants on a reasonably large scale and have given discounts ranging from 20 to 50%. The experiences of some of these people were reported in the *Daily Mail*.[3]

A very common experience was that at the beginning the tenants who became homeowners had to pay quite a bit more than their neighbours. In one case the mortgage payments came to more than twice their weekly rent – and they had to pay rates on top, previously included in the rent. But five years later, their neighbour's rent had doubled – and their mortgage payments, allowing for tax relief plus rates, were about the same as their neighbour's.

How long it takes for council rents to catch up with mortgage payments depends on the rate of increase of either: in recent years both seem to have shown a tendency to rise and rise. But mortgage payments can go down – council rents never do.

If you are older – and therefore choose to repay your mortgage over a shorter period of time (say ten to fifteen years instead of twenty-five years), this will make the mortgage payments higher and therefore delay the time before you are better off than your neighbours. Getting a high discount on the property reduces the mortgage payments – and so to a certain extent equalises the amount which older and younger council tenants have to pay. (The older ones are likely to get higher discounts as they have been council tenants longer but need to pay for a shorter term so that their mortgage is repaid by retirement age.)

Reselling

Most council tenants who buy do so not because they want to be self-reliant in retirement but because they want to own their own home and have the mobility which goes with it.[4] The snag about buying a council house or flat is that it may not be as readily resellable if it is situated on an estate which has remained predominantly council. This may depend on the characteristics of the estate – and it might be argued that it is not the fact that the estate is a council one, but rather the design and scale which puts off would-be buyers who are not already living there. There is no doubt that if the estate where you buy is small or close to the countryside, you will have less trouble. And of course if you happen to live in an isolated council house not on a council estate at all, then no one will even know it used to be a council house.

In some cases, even if there is prejudice against buying a house on a council estate, this may be remedied if a majority of tenants decide to buy. This is more likely to occur where the estate is a modern and pleasant one.

One major restriction imposed on council tenants who bought their house was that if they resold during a five year period they had to offer to resell to the council at the original sale price (plus an addition for improvements or deduction for deterioration).

Sometimes a council would agree to repayment of part of the discount instead of taking up its right to rebuy at the original price. This system will replace the 'resell' provision for all councils under the 1980 Housing Act. The buyer will have to refund a proportion of the discount for up to five years after purchase. If he sells after one year the proportion of the discount refundable will be 80%; in year two 60%; in year three 40%; in year four 20%.

However for one family, reported in the *Daily Mail*, buying their council home brought nothing but problems. Soon after buying their house, their neighbours moved and the council replaced them with a 'problem family'. They decided to sit it out until the five year period had expired but then found it impossible to sell their house. 'Once prospective buyers found it was on a council estate they did not even bother to come and look,' the family claimed.

The right to buy

In the 1980 Housing Act the right to buy will apply to a 'secure' council tenant who has been one for a total of three years – not necessarily continuously – before an application to purchase.[5] The rules apply to local councils, new town development corporations and some housing associations. A local council can sell a home to anyone else – but only 'secure' tenants can compel the council to do so.

Most council tenancies will become 'secure' tenancies. Exceptions include fixed term tenancies for more than twenty-one years (which is more like owning than renting anyway);

tenancies where the home goes with a job (e.g. school caretakers); temporary accommodation for the homeless and private sector tenants whose homes are being repaired; tenancies on land which the council acquired for development; business and licensed tenancies; tenancies to students and tenancies of less than a year provided for people who move into an area to take up an employment offer; and licences held by people who originally were squatters.

When you have a joint tenancy, both partners will have a joint right to buy. In addition the tenant buying will be allowed to buy jointly with up to three members of his family who have been living with him continuously for at least twelve months at the time he applies to buy the house or flat.

Almost all council and new town houses and flats are included in the scheme. Flats and maisonettes will be sold on a 125 year lease and will be subject to service charges and the cost of repairs being passed on to residents in the same way as private blocks of flats (see p. 100). A tenant who wants to buy his own flat may be offered another flat by the local council instead: this could be to his advantage if the council intends to put all its purchasers into one block – and to sell off complete blocks rather than leaving a mixture of council tenants and owner-occupiers which might otherwise be the case.

Tenants of certain accommodation for the elderly or disabled which has been purpose built or specially converted will not have the right to buy although councils will be able to sell if they wish.

Special conditions may apply where a council sells a house in an area of Outstanding Natural Beauty or National Park, or certain other rural areas; any subsequent sale might be restricted to someone who has lived or worked there for, say, three years. Other conditions may also be applied. In such areas if the purchaser wants to sell within ten years he may have to offer it back to the council at the then market price as judged by the District Valuer.

The market value of the house or flat will be worked out by the local council – but the tenant will have the right to appeal to the District Valuer if he thinks the value put on his home is too high. The valuation will apply to the date of the tenant's application to buy, except that in the first six months from the date of commencement of the 1980 Housing Act, the date of enactment of the bill will apply.

Mortgages and options

There is no reason why you have to get your mortgage from the council just because you are a council tenant buying a council house or flat. In fact the Government wants to encourage building societies to lend on council homes. However, council tenants in England and Wales have the right to a mortgage from the council of not less than two and a half times the tenant's income (plus one times the income of each other purchaser) or 100% of the purchase price if this is less. Joint mortgages are available with up to three other members of the household. In Scotland the right to a mortgage is available following a refusal by a building society.

If a tenant cannot get a large enough mortgage, he or she will be able to take an option to purchase the home at any time from two years following the date of the initial application at the same price. The option requires a £100 returnable deposit.

Shared ownership

Suppose you cannot afford the deposit or payments on your home. Why not buy half or a third instead? This seemingly pie in the sky solution has been used since 1975 by Birmingham City Council which sold new houses not only to tenants but also to would-be owner-occupiers who are not. Shared ownership schemes may become more common in the future as some of the obstacles to them are in the process of being removed. The stipulation that a purchaser must buy at least 50% of the home has been removed.

The most important feature of shared ownership is that the purchaser has the option to buy the remainder once he can afford to do so. The value at which this is done will be the market value at the time the option is exercised. Under the new rules being introduced, whatever proportion is bought, the purchaser will be regarded as an owner rather than a tenant and will thus have the rights and obligations of an owner even though his share may be less than 50%. Shared ownership purchases are made on a 99 or 125 year lease – though once the option to buy the remaining half has been taken up, the purchaser of a house will be able to obtain the freehold.

Homesteading scheme

This is a scheme started by the Greater London Council aimed at encouraging first time buyers who live or work in the area to renovate dilapidated houses (flats are not included in the scheme). These houses may already be owned by the council or they can be houses which the first time buyer finds for himself.

The first time buyer is expected to improve and repair the property to a standard approved by the council. The main advantage of this type of property is that it is likely to be much cheaper to buy than a comparable well looked after house in the same area.

The GLC gives a mortgage on the property and probably a renovation grant (see p. 109). In return for complying with the rules of the scheme (which are quite complicated) and also doing up the house to a good standard, the purchaser does not have to pay interest or repay any capital for the first one to three years. This enables them to live somewhere else whilst major alterations and repairs are being made. The length of time during which payments do not need to be made depends on the amount of money which needs to be spent on putting the house right. A leaflet is available from the GLC.

NOTES

1 This applies to England and Wales. Similar provisions apply to Scotland and are contained in Tenants' Rights, Etc. (Scotland) Act 1980.
2 There will be a maximum money value of discount. Also the

discounted sale price of a house first occupied after 1 April 1974 must not be less than the cost of providing the house including the cost of improvements after that date.

3   28 March 1979.

4   For how tenants can swop accommodation see Appendix 1.

5   For how to set about buying the home, see the free leaflets *The Right to Buy*, Department of Environment, Welsh Office; *Your Right to Buy Your Home*, Scottish Information Office. You also need a 'Right to Buy Claim Form'.

4

Initial Costs

In addition to finding a mortgage there are a number of other costs you will incur when buying a property. Many of these are related to the purchase price and in this chapter I have illustrated these with the example of a couple buying their first home for £25,000.

Deposit

It is rare to obtain a mortgage for 100% of the purchase price. Around 90% is the typical upper limit from a building society. So with a £25,000 house you might have to find a £3,000 deposit.

Solicitors' charges

In England and Wales there is no fixed scale of solicitors' fees although the Royal Commission on Legal Services reporting in October 1979 recommended that a maximum scale be introduced.[1] However a common charge is 1% of the purchase price plus VAT; it might be more on a cheaper property and less on a more expensive one. In an example of a £25,000 house the solicitor's fee comes to £250 plus £37.50 VAT; £150 would be cheap, £300 expensive.

There will also be the building society solicitor's fee for preparing the mortgage. It is cheaper if your own solicitor is on the building society's panel – so he can act for them and you. The large societies usually have thousands of solicitors on their panel: small ones do not and may insist they are represented by a separate solicitor. If the building society solicitor does not act for you, you will pay more for each service. The building society solicitor's charge will be 60% more than it would have been had he also been acting for you.[2] And your own solicitor will also charge a fee for dealing with the mortgage on your behalf. It will also slow things down.

The most effective way to keep a solicitor's charges down is to ask for a fixed price quotation at the outset. Many solicitors will not be prepared to work on that basis but they should at least give you an estimate, and only if your transaction turns out to be more time consuming, are they entitled to charge more.

Ask more than one firm of solicitors what they would charge and make sure that they include the building society solicitor's fee and (if applicable) have included stamp duty and land registry fees as well. Also ask whether the estimate includes VAT. You should then have a comprehensive and accurate guide to the expense involved. Unless the differences are small, go to the cheapest.

If a solicitor refuses to give you any idea of the cost, go elsewhere. Do not be afraid to haggle. There is most scope for shopping around if you are buying or selling an expensive house – there is no more work, but many solicitors tend to relate the fee to the value of the house. In May 1977 *Which?* reported that one of its members had asked at least six solicitors for quotes on the same transaction. These ranged from £60 to £300 – their member paid £60.

Once you have agreed terms with a solicitor it is best to confirm them in writing so there can be no misunderstanding. Another way of saving on legal costs is to go to cut price conveyancing firms or to do the conveyancing yourself. This is discussed in Chapter 7.

When the transaction is completed sometimes a solicitor charges more than his estimate. If his account exceeds the estimate by a significant amount, say £50 or more, ring him up and ask him why – if he has not already explained. In England and Wales[3] if you are not satisfied with his answer, do not pay the bill but instead write to your solicitor requesting that he obtain a Remuneration Certificate from the Law Society. If you do this, the solicitor sends the papers to the Law Society which certifies either that the bill is reasonable or else fixes a *lower* sum. If you pay the bill you lose your rights to have the Law Society check the bill unless the solicitor deducts it from any money he owes you. You can ask for a Remuneration Certificate even if the solicitor does not exceed his estimate if you think you have been overcharged. In 1976 the Law Society said they reduced about a quarter of the bills sent to them but most people did not query their bills.

Land registry fees

In England and Wales most houses are now registered at one of the regional land registries or will have to be registered when you buy. When a registered house or flat is transferred (or first registered), fees have to be paid by the purchaser and the solicitor pays them on your behalf. This adds another £62 to our specimen bill; the more expensive the property the larger the fee. At the time of writing land registry fees amounted to roughly $\frac{1}{4}\%$ of the purchase price on a transfer.

The fees for a first registration are lower – but your solicitor will have more work so he may charge more than he otherwise would. No land registry fee is payable to register a mortgage taken out at the same time as a purchase. A solicitor should be able to tell you how much the land registry fees will be. There is no VAT on land registry fees.

Stamp duty

Stamp duty is payable to the Inland Revenue by purchasers on the whole value of the property where the purchase price is above certain limits. These limits are changed from time to time. From 6 April 1980 there is no stamp duty on properties bought for £20,000 or less; from £20,001 to £25,000 the rate is ½%; from £25,001 to £30,000 it is 1%; from £30,001 to £35,000 it is 1½%; £35,001 and over it is 2%. When a new lease is granted the amount of stamp duty is determined by the ground rent not the purchase price.

If the asking price is near one of these limits, try and bargain the price down. For instance if the price is £20,950 and you get it down to £20,000, you need pay nothing instead of £104.75. But if you only bargain it down to £20,050 the stamp duty is still £100.25. Check with your solicitor what the correct rates are at the time you are buying.

There is no stamp duty payable on moveable things you buy with the house – fittings, carpets, etc., if you agree a separate price for them. In such a situation you should ask your solicitor to suggest the seller agrees to 'apportion' the price; so you might pay £20,000 for the house – and £950 for fixtures, carpets, etc. Stamp duty would then amount to nothing, i.e. the same as on a £20,000 purchase.

Inspection and survey fees

Before the building society even offers you a loan it will want a cheque for its inspection fee. This is on a scale based on the price of the house – not the amount of the loan. The only scope to haggle with the building society over this is if the mortgage is a very low proportion of the price – say less than a third. On a £25,000 purchase it would cost about £47 including VAT.[2]

In addition a full structural survey could cost around £100 (see p. 28 for advice on choosing a surveyor).

Removal, decorations, furniture

Allow another £100 to £300 for removal expenses. Even if you do it yourself you will probably have to hire a mini-van and throw a house warming party for the friends who helped you; also make sure you are insured for breakages in transit although

Table 5   Check list of costs for £25,000 purchase with £22,000 Mortgage

		Your cost	Example
1	Your deposit	£......	£3 000
2	Solicitor's fee for conveyancing[1]	£......	£287
3	Solicitor's fee for mortgage[1]	£......	£63
4	Land registry fees	£......	£62
5	Stamp duty	£......	£125
6	Building society inspection fee	£......	£47
7	Structural survey	£......	£100
8	Removal expenses[1]	£......	£100
9	Decorating, repairs etc.[1]	£......	£200
10	Furniture, carpets etc.[1]	£......	£600
11	Anything else [2]	£......	
	Total funds you need in addition to mortgage	£......	£4 584

[1] Including VAT.
[2] For example: solicitor's costs, estate agent's charges if you are selling as well as buying.

they may be less likely to occur if you are doing it yourself. If you employ a professional firm you will pay less if you do your own packing. Get quotes from two or three firms and compare them with the cost (and trouble) of doing it yourself.

You will probably want to redecorate inside and perhaps out. Even a place which looks quite clean with its old furniture in place tends to look rather shabby after the pictures have been taken off the walls. And unless it is a new house the surveyor may find repairs which need to be seen to. Indeed the building society may insist on these being done as a condition of the loan. I have allowed £200 for this.

You may also find that once you get your own home you want to buy a lot of 'once and for all' items which now seem essential but which you never thought you would need when you rented or lived with your parents. A home has to be furnished. If you are lucky you will buy one with fitted carpets and curtains which you like. Sometimes even the cooker and fridge are left. You may get presents of course; and it is amazing what good value second-hand furniture is if you just cannot afford new. Make sure you have at least £500 to spare (or a good credit limit on your credit card) to cope with this extra expenditure.

Add another £100 for the 'light fittings' which the seller now says were not included originally – and we find we need a deposit of £4,584 – more than half as much again as the £3,000 first thought of. My figures are just an example of course – so you should carefully work out for yourself what your initial costs will be.

NOTES

1 In Scotland there is a scale of charges (see p. 83).
2 The Building Society solicitor's fee is on a scale agreed between the Law Society and the Building Societies' Association. The scale and other costs are published by the latter in a free booklet *Building Societies and House Purchase*. The solicitor's mortgage fee is based on the amount of the advance. It is roughly $\frac{1}{4}\%$.
3 If you are dissatisfied with a Scottish solicitor's charges you are entitled to have his bill submitted to 'taxation' by the Auditor of the Court of Session (even after you have paid it) but you will have to pay the cost of the taxation and the Auditor can raise the bill as well as lower it.

5

Finding a Mortgage

A mortgage is a loan secured on your home. If you do not repay
the loan in the way you have agreed the lender can apply to a
Court to sell your property to get his money back.

Building societies provide the vast majority of mortgages for
owner-occupation, in some years as many as nine out of ten.
Rules about how much you can borrow are therefore based on
building society practice – but other lenders, such as local
authorities, insurance companies and banks are likely to behave
in much the same way.[1]

Advance planning

Choosing a building society

Many building societies will only lend to people who have
invested their savings with them, especially when funds are in
short supply, as they often are.[2] So if you think you might want a
mortgage, you would be wise to plan in advance and keep as
much money as you can in one or more building societies.
Preferably more than one, because some societies are fussier than
others about the type of property on which they lend. Also when
funds are in short supply they ration them in different ways.

There is no point, however, in spreading your money too thinly or at the last minute – if your account has only £50 in it, or you have only had it a few months, no society is going to think much of that. What they like to see is regular saving or large balances. So you could save regularly with one society – subscription accounts pay high interest rates – and keep any lump sum you have in an ordinary or 'share' account with another.

Choosing the right building society to save with presents a problem for someone who later wants to take out a mortgage with that society. This is because building societies rarely talk openly about the conditions under which they lend. The larger societies now have leaflets available on request which summarise their mortgage terms – it is well worth while getting hold of a copy before you start saving.

These rules do change from time to time however. One couple I heard of moved all but £20 of their savings from one building society to another because they discovered they could get a larger loan provided they saved for six months. At the end of six months they were aghast to discover that the new society had changed its rules – and would now only lend to investors who had been with them for eighteen months. They went back to the first society which offered them the mortgage they needed. Their attempt to beat the system had done them no good at all.

Homeloan scheme

This scheme was introduced by the Government in 1978 and anyone who has never owned a home before (i.e. any prospective first time buyer) should pick up the appropriate notification form and join. Savings under the scheme need not be newly commenced nor be with a building society – National Savings Bank, bank deposit accounts and National Savings Index-Linked SAYE also qualify. After two years in the scheme when you apply for a mortgage (which does not have to be the institution with which you have registered under the scheme), you should be able to benefit from an extra tax free bonus and up to an extra £600 loan on which you will not have to pay interest or repay any capital for the first five years.

The snags are that your home must cost less than a figure from a regional list which will be updated from time to time. From 1 December 1980 the limits range from £16,400 to £29,100. Also you need to have £600 in the account when you ask for the mortgage, and an average of £300 over the previous twelve months. And there is a maximum tax free bonus. But it costs you nothing to join – and the conditions may have varied by the time you come to buy your home. It is therefore well worth joining – and anyway you can lose nothing even if you don't eventually qualify. There is a free explanatory leaflet.[3]

How much they will lend you

Building societies usually lend a multiple of your before tax earnings. If you receive regular spare-time earnings or overtime, they may also be prepared to take these into account – but they will want proof. If you or your spouse have investment income – and are not going to put all the capital into the house purchase – this may also be taken into account. The multiple might be two to three times your income. So if your income is £6,000 a year you should be able to borrow between £12,000 and £18,000. When interest rates are high, the multiple tends to be lower.

Many young couples buy their first home when they are both earning. While two societies may give the same amount to a sole earner there is less uniformity when there are two. The Sex Discrimination Act, 1975 makes it unlawful for building societies to discriminate against women. And nowadays it should be no more difficult for a single woman to get the mortgage she wants than a single man. However couples, where the wife has higher earnings than the husband, may find they are not offered as much as they would be if their earning capacities were reversed. This tendency was demonstrated by a survey[4] which found that in spite of the assertion by building society head offices that there is no discrimination whatever, this turned out not to be so in practice. The survey also showed that the amounts offered could vary very greatly between societies and even between different branches of the same society as illustrated in Table 6.

Take the example of Bob and Mary. With Bob earning £6,000 and Mary earning £3,000, a society which gave two and a half times Bob's earnings plus Mary's earnings would provide them with a loan of £18,000. Another society might have a rule of thumb that it lends three times the higher income – and ignores the lower – which in this case also gives £18,000. But

Table 6   Size of mortgage offered: higher earner £3,650; lower earner £2,400

	Biggest £	Average £	Smallest £
Husband had higher earnings	15 000	11 720	7 900
Wife had higher earnings	14 550	11 250	5 500

Source: Equal Opportunities Commission/Consumers Association Survey 1978.

had Bob and Mary both been on £4,500, then they would only have got £13,500 from that society. A third might give two and a half times the higher plus two and a half times half the lower – that would give a mortgage of £18,750. Another formula might be to give twice the higher and twice the lower – again £18,000 in Bob and Mary's example.

Whether or not there are two earners, should you have large hire purchase or credit card commitments, other existing debts, pay maintenance to a separated or former wife – or have to support children who are not living with you, you might be offered less. So do not necessarily volunteer this information; if you are asked, as you often will be, you must of course tell the truth. Regular spare-time earnings or overtime ought to be taken into account but sometimes will not be – it rather depends on what the building society manager knows about the type of job you are in.

The self-employed may find greater difficulty in getting a large enough mortgage in current inflationary times. This is because most societies require to see the last three years' audited accounts – and some may take an average of them – a much more conservative basis than for an employed person. Someone who has recently set up in business on his own will find it difficult – even impossible – to get a building society mortgage. People who run family businesses through a company may find societies less willing to accept their salary in full.

Not all building societies are willing to give a mortgage to two single people jointly. A few will lend a joint mortgage to two couples if they want to share.

Building society managers have discretion to vary the rules a bit – but for first time buyers it is often not their income which determines how much the building society will lend them, but the property they have chosen.

Do not overstretch yourself

Having given advice on how to set about getting the highest possible mortgage it is appropriate here to warn about the dangers of overstretching yourself. Any house purchaser should always keep some cash in reserve for unforeseen eventualities.

You should also be careful not to offer evidence of overtime earnings if there is a chance your overtime might dry up – or worse if you are in line to lose your job. Lenders make the loans based on a maximum multiple of your income for the very good reason that they have found from experience that on a lower income people often cannot afford the mortgage payments.

Remember also if your wife is earning but is likely to stop work to have a baby before long, that is going to sharply reduce your income. Low start mortgages might be avoided for the same reason as the higher payments later may coincide with the arrival of a family and drop in income when the wife stops working.

How much they will lend on the property

You may have worked out that your income is ample to support a mortgage of the amount you need. But if the loan you seek is over 80% of the price you are paying, you may hit another snag.

Building societies always make an inspection and valuation; sometimes this valuation is less than the price you have agreed to pay. For instance although you might think you have a bargain at £25,000, the building society valuer may well reckon the value is £24,000. Most societies have a lending limit in terms of the percentage of valuation above which they will not lend. The £22,000 our example couple needs is 92% of the £24,000 which the Heartless Permanent's surveyor valued their intended home. But Heartless applies its 90% lending limit and offers £21,500 – in fact just under 90% of valuation.

The lending limit tends to vary according to the age, state of repair and type of house. Some societies lend lower proportions on more expensive houses. For houses built before 1920 this limit can be as low as 70% of valuation; for modern houses it can range from 80–95%. Mortgages of 100% of the purchase price rarely occur – usually when the purchaser is buying for less than the valuation: a sitting tenant could be in such a position (see p. 137).

Disliked property

Building societies as a whole seem to be against certain types of property although the societies do vary in outlook. Converted flats used to be almost impossible to get building society mortgages on; now there are few large societies which actually say 'No' point blank. However old habits die hard and if a converted flat is what you are after – they are mainly to be found in London – then you should know that the Halifax, Abbey National and Nationwide, the three largest societies, say they do not put extra obstacles in the way of people who want to live in this sort of flat.

Some (but by no means all) building societies do not like

houses without gardens – though a small patio might be okay; flats without gardens are fine. Others will not lend on homes partially occupied by sitting tenants, or on homes without bathrooms (some will not lend even if you agree to put one in) or on homes with outside toilets only.

Leasehold property is expected by societies to have a lease with from twenty to thirty years still to run *after* you have paid off the mortgage, i.e. a minimum forty-five to fifty-five years in the case of a standard twenty-five year mortgage. Freehold flats are difficult to get mortgages on because there cannot be enforceable agreements between the residents on how repairs, maintenance, etc., are carried out and who pays for them.

Where a property is in need of fairly substantial repairs, a lender will withold some of the loan. This is called a 'retention' and will generally amount to the estimated cost of the repairs which you need to carry out. Should the repairs be very extensive – a new roof, say – then the society withholds the whole loan until the repairs are completed. In either case a bank would normally be prepared to provide a bridging loan once you are able to show them a formal written offer from the building society.

Additional security

As well as having a maximum percentage of the valuation above which building societies will not lend at all, they also have a 'normal' limit above which they require extra security. In fact they always insist on extra security for any loan in excess of 80% of their valuation. This security can be one of the following:

1 A special insurance policy called a mortgage indemnity or guarantee policy which costs you 3 to 4% of the amount in excess of 80%. The cost of the mortgage indemnity policy can usually be added to your loan – it is a single non-recurring premium. In our example our couple need a mortgage indemnity policy to cover the difference between £19,200 (80% of the society's £24,000 valuation) and £21,500 which they are borrowing. The cost is £80 which the society adds to

their loan.[5] This policy is completely different from a mortgage protection policy – see Chapter 6.

2   They could instead use a life insurance policy which has been going long enough to have a surrender value to cover the £2,300 above 80% which needs extra security. Young people often have such policies but they frequently do not have a large enough combined surrender value.

3   A mortgage on another property. This might cost as much in extra legal and land registry fees as the mortgage indemnity policy – so check whether it is worthwhile. It also has the disadvantage of tying up the other property.

4   A guarantee from a local Council under the Housing Act 1980.

Mortgage not big enough

Having got to the stage of being offered a building society mortgage you may find you still have not got enough money. In Chapter 4 I set out a checklist of initial costs. Our couple Bob and Mary thought they needed £4,584 in addition to the building society mortgage. But because of the lower valuation put on their house by the building society valuer they now need a further £500.

They tried to get the price down but the sellers were not prepared to budge having already come down £500. Bob and Mary did not like the idea of using up their entire credit card limits on furniture; they would like to go on holiday the year after they moved – and without saving the credit card for that there would be no way.

This is where their endowment policies proved useful. Both had been paying premiums for a few years and between them they found that the insurance companies would lend them £350 on the security of their policies. They also went to Bob's bank manager and when they offered the security of the policies and showed him the letters from the insurance companies, he agreed to lend them the full £500. He took the insurance policies as security and told them there was no need for any more security as he was impressed by the way they managed their affairs. He did add he would like them to pay off the loan within five years – whereas the insurance companies would have waited until the maturity of the policies. But they agreed all the same because the alternative was credit card or hire purchase for the furniture which would be much more expensive.

In fact Bob and Mary's bank manager might have been prepared to lend them more and if the £4,584 was all the money they had in the world, they would be sensible to borrow at this stage because they could get tax relief on the bank loan to help to buy the house but not on a loan to buy a new car or go on holiday (see p. 123).

For people who cannot offer security such as life insurance policies, shares or unit trusts, banks will often take a second mortgage as security for a 'top-up' loan.

A second mortgage is given where a lender is prepared to take your property as security but agrees that the first mortgage should have priority if you do not keep up the payments. It is not as good security as a first mortgage which is why a second mortgage will be at a higher rate of interest.

Insurance companies also provide quite a lot of top-up loans. The snag often is that they require you to take out and keep up an expensive insurance policy to cover not just the top-up portion which they are lending you, but also the amount lent by your building society. Such arrangements, particularly where the amount to be topped up is small in relation to the total loan, should be avoided if at all possible – they turn out very expensive. If you do resort to a top-up loan from an insurance company, ask whether the building society loan can be linked to a lower cost endowment policy. Not all companies give this choice, insisting you take a full with-profits or non-profit policy for the amount of the combined value of your building society and top-up loan. For an explanation of why a lower cost is preferable, see p. 65. Insurance companies require a second mortgage as well as these insurance policies.

Interest rates

The basic mortgage rate charged by building societies has for some years been decided by the Building Societies Association – and all building societies of any significance abide by its decisions. Nowadays few lenders charge a fixed rate of interest – they can raise or lower it by giving you a month's notice – or increasingly without notice although you do not necessarily need to alter your monthly payments at once. Local authorities often used to charge fixed rates of interest – this is no longer the case for new mortgages. Some insurance companies still offer fixed rates of interest; with others the rate is reviewed after five years.

Most building societies work out the amount of interest for the year based on the amount of money you owe at the beginning of that year. But if you have a repayment mortgage you repay some of the capital each month. So the average amount of money you owe during the year is less than the amount on which interest is worked out. This means your monthly payments on a building society loan at say 12% interest could be more than those on a 12% repayment mortgage from a bank. Or to put it another way the true rate of interest on a 12% building society mortgage is about $12\frac{3}{4}\%$.

Endowment mortgages have no repayment of capital each month. The mortgage is paid off when the policy matures. So the rate quoted on an endowment mortgage is the true rate – societies generally charge $\frac{1}{4}\%$ or $\frac{1}{2}\%$ more for these. So an endowment mortgage would be at $12\frac{1}{4}\%$ or $12\frac{1}{2}\%$ interest where a repayment mortgage is quoted at 12%.

Increasingly societies are charging more for large loans of perhaps £15,000 to £20,000. The extra charged for large loans ranges from $\frac{1}{2}\%$ to $1\frac{1}{2}\%$. A handful of societies charge extra if the home is old or unusual. So when the basic building society mortgage rate is announced as 12% some people will be paying 14% or more.

Other lenders

Local authorities

Local authority mortgages are often in short supply because the local authorities are restricted by the government as to how much they are allowed to lend.

Local authorities differ in their rules about where and to whom they will lend. The authority to enquire at is the one in which you currently live – and the one into which you are moving. If you live in Greater London or are moving into part of it, you might have a third choice of the Greater London Council. In Northern Ireland instead of local authorities, you apply to the Northern Ireland Housing Executive.

Local authorities tend to work out how much they will lend to you in a different way from most building societies – although the actual loan may be about the same. They reckon that your before tax weekly income should be enough to cover your monthly outgoings. Monthly outgoings means your mortgage payments usually ignoring tax relief. As the payments on an option mortgage are lower than the before tax relief payments on an ordinary repayment mortgage, a local authority may therefore lend you more if you take an option mortgage. There is no logic in this attitude as the after tax relief cost of a repayment mortgage in the early years is in fact less than with an option mortgage. Some other lenders may include ground rent, rates or even heavy hire purchase commitments in your monthly outgoings. If there are two incomes, the higher and say half the lower may be taken into account.

Local authority mortgages are intended to be lent on cheaper housing so there is usually a maximum price of home they will contemplate lending on. These limits are raised from time to time. They also tend to restrict loans to older (pre-1939) houses. In 1978 93% of GLC mortgages and 84% of other English local authority mortgages were on houses built before 1919 compared with only 23% of building society mortgages.[6]

In fact the council tries to step in when building societies are not interested. Often a building society refusal to lend on a certain property is required before a council will consider lending. Interest rates are similar to those of building societies.

In times when councils are very short of mortgage funds, building societies have agreed to consider council nominations. However this will not help with a property or a borrower unacceptable to a society as the building societies have not agreed to lower their standards for council nominations.

A council is more likely than any other lender to grant a 100% mortgage. In 1978 38% of GLC and 22% of other local authority mortgages were for 100% or more of the price compared with only 1% of building society mortgages.[6] In spite of the fact that there are so many more building society than local authority mortgages available in total, you are nearly twice as likely to get a 100% mortgage from a local authority than from a building society.

Insurance companies

You are more likely to get a top-up mortgage than a full loan from an insurance company. Either way it will turn out rather expensive for the reasons already given and explained further in Chapter 6. A mortgage or insurance broker is the best person to fix you up with an insurance company loan if you can find no cheaper means of financing your purchase; the Corporation of Mortgage Finance and Life Assurance Brokers will let you have the names of members in your area. Several magazines carry out surveys of insurance company mortgages and top-up facilities.[7]

Banks

All the main banks, Barclays, Lloyds, National Westminster, Midland and the TSB now offer mortgages for house purchase on terms of up to twenty-five years. Although their quoted interest rate appears to be higher due to differences in the way banks and building societies work out their interest, at the beginning of 1981 bank loans were hardly, if any, more expensive than building society ones. Banks may also lend more to the self employed. Some banks see lending as a chance to sell you an endowment insurance policy which you might not otherwise want. However as banks act as brokers themselves you could get a better choice of policy than by going direct to an insurance company. Interest on a bank mortgage is often 2% above the current bank base rate. Check whether there is an 'arrangement' fee. A few finance companies and foreign banks also lend for house purchase – usually at even higher rates of interest.

Employers
Some employers offer staff low interest loans. This is most common in banks, insurance companies and building societies for obvious reasons.

Many large companies also have arrangements for introductions to building societies and insurance companies which can help you jump a queue. Employers of people in the trade, such as solicitors, accountants and estate agents will also find doors open more easily.

Speeding things up

The only way to ensure you get a mortgage for more or less the amount you want is never to give up. Even if you have made advance plans by spreading your savings between two building societies, do not hesitate to move the money away to a third if their response to your enquiry is more encouraging. But make sure you speak to the right person – if you do not think what you have been told sounds right, write and ask for a written explanation of why they cannot lend.

Using contacts

Apart from doing your own footwork from branch to branch, always take advantage of your contacts. Bank managers, estate agents, solicitors, accountants, insurance brokers and insurance company agents all have influence with building societies. They recommend people to deposit money and in return are given a quota to be lent to their clients. Often the client need not even have an account with the society. Try to make sure any promises made to you are of substance. And check whether they charge an arrangement fee.

Insurance brokers and agents will want you to take out an endowment policy. But solicitors will not necessarily. If you do take one, the solicitor may be prepared to cut his conveyancing fees to take into account the commission he received on the insurance policy. If you do not have your own solicitor, as well as his fees and whether you like him, it may be as important to choose one who can get you a mortgage.

Mortgage brokers

As their name implies, mortgage brokers are in business to get people mortgages. Nowadays they all have to be licensed.[8] Especially when mortgages are in short supply they undoubtedly perform a very useful task for those who otherwise could not find one. They will generally find you a building society or insurance company mortgage and you will normally be expected to take an endowment mortgage. The commission on the endowment policy serves to pay the broker for his work.

Whether or not you should have an endowment mortgage is discussed in the next chapter. If the loan is from a building society (rather than an insurance company) you should be given the choice of paying the broker a fee instead of taking an endowment mortgage. You should make sure you know what the fee is beforehand.[9] A typical mortgage broker's fee will be around 2% of the mortgage – so a £22,000 mortgage could cost you up to £440. But remember if the broker found you a loan for £2,000 more than you could have got yourself, you will have to put down £2,000 less towards the deposit – and should not therefore begrudge him the money.

The broker may ask for a fee in advance. You should *not* agree to this – if pressed, offer a part payment. Remember if you meanwhile find a loan elsewhere and do not want the one he finds, the maximum he can charge by law is £1 if you do not take up his introduction within six months. Where the loan is over £5,000 the broker is entitled to charge you for any surveys, etc., he has had done on your behalf.

Bridging loans

Generally speaking you are advised not to sign a contract to buy a new home before you have also signed to sell your old one.

If for some reason you do and have to finalise the purchase of the new one before you have the proceeds from the old one, you will need a bridging loan. You may also need a bridging loan if there is some delay in getting your mortgage.

There are also two situations where you may need a bridging loan to cover part or all of the deposit.

The first applies to first time buyers who are offered a mortgage of over 90% of the purchase price. They will need to pay a 10% deposit when the contract is signed whilst their contribution to the purchase price of the home may only be, say, 5%. The building society will not cough up any money until the deal is completed, usually a month later. In this case it is worth asking the vendor's solicitor to accept a smaller deposit.

The second occurs when you are selling as well as buying but do not intend to put any capital into the new house other than what you are realising from the old one. Say you are selling for £20,000 and buying a new house for £30,000. You have to put up a £3,000 deposit – but that £3,000 is tied up in your old house. You will not normally be able to use the £2,000 deposit paid to your solicitor by the purchaser of your old house because he holds it as 'stakeholder' which means he cannot pass it on to you without permission from your purchaser – which is unlikely to be forthcoming.

In any of these cases you should go and see your bank manager. Be quite definite about how long you will require it – usually the shorter the period the easier it is. You may be surprised how accommodating bank managers can be.

Provided you have a solicitor acting for you, he can hold the deeds of one of your two houses 'to the order of the bank' and so give them security for your bridging loan. If you use a conveyancing company or are doing-it-yourself, a bridging loan will be more difficult to get.

Ask the bank manager what rate of interest he charges and whether there is a fee as well. If there is, and the loan is for a short period, try bartering with him on this. Should your bank manager not be amenable to a bridging loan, this could be the moment to change banks. The same applies if his fee is high; some banks do not charge fees for bridging loans – just interest. You do not get tax relief on a fee for a bridging loan – only on the interest. And remember the fee will often be payable even if you do not take up the loan.

NOTES

1   In 1977 in England some 10% of first time buyers did not need to borrow at all; 77% got loans from building societies; 6% from local authorities; 3% from banks; 2% from insurance companies; 2% private loans; and 1% other loans, according to the Department of Environment National Movers Survey.

2   The Bradford & Bingley Building Society guarantees mortgages for investors saving for at least two years at a reduced interest rate under its 'Homebuilder Scheme'.

3   *Homeloan, Special Help for First Time Buyers*, Department of Environment.

4   Equal Opportunities Commission/Consumers Association, 1978.

5   If you are buying a low priced house you may be eligible for a cheaper mortgage indemnity policy and a 100% mortgage under the Option Mortgage Guarantee Scheme. See the free leaflet *Buying Your House on an Option Mortgage*, Department of Environment.

6   *The 20% Sample Survey of Local Authority Mortgages*, Department of Environment, 1979.

7   See *Planned Savings*; *Money Management*; *Mortgage & Insurance Review*, Corporation of Mortgage Brokers.

8   By the Office of Fair Trading, Consumer Credit Division.

9   Members of the Corporation of Mortgage, Finance and Life Assurance Brokers are bound to do this by their Code of Conduct.

6

Repaying a Mortgage

Why is it that some people seem to find repaying their mortgage such a financial burden whilst others seem to take it in their stride? The reason lies not in the size of the loan you get; you will not get much more than three times your income – however confident you are that you can afford the repayments. It lies in the type of mortgage you choose. For the same size of loan, you can find yourself paying widely different amounts each month. It is therefore crucial not to be persuaded into getting a more expensive mortgage than you need.

The two main types of mortgages are repayment and endowment. As well as ordinary full repayment mortgages there are low start repayment mortgages and option repayment mortgages (where you pay lower interest instead of getting tax relief). There are also several types of endowment mortgages which vary greatly in cost.

Repayment mortgages

With a repayment mortgage you pay interest and also repay some of the capital each month. The amount of each combined payment depends on the rate of interest at the time and the initial term over which you have chosen to repay.[1] The payment is fixed at the outset by the lender but can vary in the future as rates of interest vary. You can get tax relief on the interest but not on the capital. There are four types of repayment mortgage: full repayment, option, low start and high start.

Full repayment mortgage

With a full repayment mortgage your monthly payments will stay the same providing the rate of interest does not vary. At the beginning of the mortgage your payment consists mostly of interest and there is only a little capital repaid. As time goes by, you gradually repay the loan. Therefore in later years less of your payment consists of interest and more of capital. In theory in later years the cost after tax relief should rise – because your monthly payment consists of more capital (on which there is no tax relief) and less interest. But when interest rates are high, say 11% or more, the interest component does not decrease significantly for many years so the cost after tax relief increases only marginally. By the time the increase bites you may have moved house and started another mortgage.

Option mortgage

An option mortgage is much the same as a full repayment mortgage except that instead of getting tax relief on the interest, you pay a lower rate of interest. The reduction in the rate of interest is broadly equivalent to the tax relief a basic rate tax-payer gets on a repayment mortgage. It is refunded to building societies by the Government. The option mortgage is unaffected by tax relief, so there are no deductions to make from the monthly payments and the cost is level throughout the term unless the interest rate changes. Option mortgages are designed for people who do not earn enough to get full tax relief.

Once you have started an option mortgage you have to wait one year before you can change it to an ordinary repayment mortgage and you have to give the lender notice before 31 December for the change to take place on the following 1 April.

If you have an ordinary mortgage and want to change it to an option mortgage, this used to be at the lender's discretion. However proposals in the Housing Act 1980 will change these rules and make it easier to switch from an option to a tax relief mortgage and vice versa. There is a free leaflet available.[2]

Low start or deferred interest repayment mortgages

The Deferred Payment Mortgage Scheme[3] is aimed at first time buyers who borrow from local authorities and building societies. It is restricted to people who are buying low cost homes and who have relatively low incomes. It is only a voluntary scheme – so you should enquire whether your proposed lender operates it and whether you and your chosen home qualify.

With this scheme your monthly payments in the first year are approximately 20% less than they would be with an ordinary repayment mortgage. For example[4] for every £1,000 of loan your net monthly payment after tax relief might be reduced from £7.13 to £6.03. These amounts rise each year until the end of the fifth year when you start paying what you would have paid in year one with an ordinary repayment mortgage. From year six to ten you pay the same as with an ordinary repayment mortgage – and from year eleven to the end you pay more. However by then your income will no doubt have risen and the extra payments will no longer be onerous.

The deferred payment mortgage is also available as an option mortgage. Either way if you qualify, it is strongly recommended. Some building societies operate their own low start mortgages and may not be as restrictive as the government scheme – but they will be looking for people who have career prospects and the expectation of a rising salary scale.

High start mortgages

Most building societies will let you pay more if you wish. This has the effect of reducing the mortgage term. The idea is that if a wife stops work to have a baby, then at that point the mortgage term can be extended and the payments reduced. Choosing at the outset to pay more for a shorter term might be a good ploy if you expect the mortgage rate to rise and you do not want to pay more then. Be certain your society will allow you to do this as nowadays many require higher payments whenever the interest rate is raised.

Mortgage protection policies

It seems prudent to make sure that if you were to die, you have enough life insurance to pay off the mortgage. A special cheap policy called a mortgage protection policy is designed to do just this and automatically pays off whatever you owe if you die before you have finished repaying your mortgage. It is sensible to have such a policy with whichever of the four repayment mortgages you choose.

If you have a joint mortgage with both partners earning, it can be a good idea to take out a joint mortgage protection policy. This pays out if either of you dies – and is cheaper than taking two separate policies.

Premiums can be paid monthly or yearly. If you take out another form of life insurance, say a family income benefit policy, at the same time from the same company and pay the premiums together, you can usually get a discount. Mortgage protection policies can be obtained through building societies, insurance brokers, banks or direct from insurance companies.

Endowment mortgages

With an endowment mortgage you pay only interest on the loan. There is no repayment of capital so your monthly payments to the lender are lower than with a repayment mortgage. However you must also pay premiums on an endowment life insurance policy which is large enough, when it matures, to pay off your loan. The lender takes the insurance policy as security as well as your home. The lender may be a building society or it might be the insurance company itself. An endowment policy also pays off the loan if you die early – so there is no need for a mortgage protection policy as well.

There are three types of endowment insurance policy which can be linked to an endowment mortgage. They are full with-profits, lower cost with-profits and non-profit.

Full with-profits endowment

As well as a guarantee to pay out a sum to exactly repay your mortgage at the end of the term, or if you die earlier, a full with-profits policy also pays you profits. By the end of the term you expect these profits (added yearly or three yearly as bonuses to the sum insured) to increase to considerably more than what you will need to repay your loan.

The only catch to this formula is that you have to pay high premiums for the endowment policy. A full with-profits policy is therefore an additional means of saving which you may not be able to afford in the early years of a mortgage.

Nowadays a full with-profits endowment mortgage makes the burden of repaying a mortgage very heavy indeed in the early years. I would therefore not recommend it unless you already happen to have such a policy in existence. If you have, you should try to get a building society to agree to a part repayment and part endowment mortgage using your existing policy as security for the endowment part. This way you will have lower payments than with a full repayment mortgage.

Lower cost with-profits endowment

A lower cost (or low cost) with-profits endowment policy is one specially designed for mortgages. It has much lower premiums than a full with-profits policy – often about half. A lower cost policy does not guarantee to pay off the loan on maturity of the policy. But the insurance company has worked out that with the addition of profits over the years as bonuses it will do – and also

leave a little spare cash for you. What it does guarantee is that if
you die before the policy matures, all the loan will be paid off.
Most people who take out endowment mortgages nowadays use
a lower cost with-profits policy.

There are some seventy different lower cost policies to choose
from. These are surveyed regularly in specialist magazines.[5]
These surveys show the monthly premium and an estimate by
the company of how it expects the policy to do in the future.
Some show how well an ordinary with-profits policy did in the
past. It is well worth while getting hold of one of these surveys
before you choose a policy.

If you want to keep the cost down at the beginning choose
from the companies with the lowest premiums. Also consider one
of the few policies where the premiums start extra low and increase.

You also need to know if your building society will accept the
policy you choose. This information is given for the largest
societies in the surveys. Otherwise ask the building society.

Non-profit endowment
A non-profit endowment policy guarantees to pay out a sum
exactly equal to the amount you need to repay your mortgage at
the end of the term or if you die earlier. The premiums on such a
policy are relatively low but there are no profits. Premiums and
interest payments come to somewhat more than the cost of a
repayment mortgage and you get no extra bonus of profits on
maturity. In practice having a non-profit policy may turn out no
different than paying a much greater rate of interest.

It is rare for anyone to take a non-profit endowment mortgage
by choice. Usually they only apply where an insurance company
insists on it as a condition for granting a loan. And if nobody else
will lend to you, then you have no choice. They are best avoided.

The costs of the different types of insurance policies to which
you can link a mortgage are summarised in Table 7.

Which type of mortgage for you

An option mortgage is aimed at people who do not have high enough incomes to get full income tax relief. People who pay the basic rate of tax are better off if they choose a full repayment mortgage instead of an option mortgage as the payments for them after tax relief are lower in the early years.

Table 7 Monthly cost of different life policies for £10,000 mortgage

Age at start of mortgage	Mortgage protection	Lower cost with-profits endowment	Full with-profits endowment	Non-profit endowment
	£	£	£	£
25	1.02	12.10	28.30	15.32
30	1.38	12.32	28.49	15.49
35	2.09	12.81	28.96	15.86
40	3.32	13.70	29.84	16.58
45	4.15	20.30	38.50	23.32
50	5.17	31.68	52.14	34.82

Source : Equitable Life. After tax relief at 17½% for twenty-five year term or to age sixty-five if earlier for man in good health. From 6 April 1981 tax relief will be reduced to 15%. Policies from other companies may cost more.

You may find an option mortgage slightly more convenient as it saves the trouble of claiming tax relief (see Chapter 12). If you need a 100% mortgage, having an option mortgage may be the only way you can get one.[6]

It is the choice between repayment and endowment which causes most confusion. You are likely to meet totally contradictory advice.

People who push endowment mortgages are usually insurance brokers, mortgage brokers and agents of insurance companies. This is because they earn a large part of their living from selling the endowment policies which go with these mortgages. Others such as solicitors, building societies and their managers, bank managers, accountants and estate agents may also be swayed by the high commission they can receive from an insurance company on such policies. A handful of insurance companies pay no commission.

For most people there is not a lot to choose between a full repayment and a lower cost endowment. On balance I think a full repayment mortgage is a more sensible choice – especially for first time buyers – for more than one reason.

First a repayment mortgage beats an endowment mortgage for flexibility. When the mortgage rate goes up, some societies do not insist that you pay more on your repayment mortgage. Instead you can extend the term or pay interest only until (hopefully) the rate goes down again. With an endowment mortgage you have to pay the increased interest each time the rate changes. An endowment mortgage term cannot be extended.

Alternatively a few building societies have a system where repayment mortgage holders need only change their payments once a year, even if interest rates change more frequently. And if you fall on hard times you can convert a repayment mortgage to an option mortgage.

Secondly even with a lower cost endowment mortgage, the cost of insurance premiums plus interest – allowing for tax relief – are always higher than the payments on a repayment mortgage at the start – and for quite a long time during the period when you can least spare the extra. This also applies even if you pay higher rates of tax – and therefore get more tax relief. The higher the interest rate and the lower the tax rate, the less attractive an endowment mortgage becomes.

Eventually the repayment mortgage is more expensive. This is because the interest part of the payments goes down year by year – and so does the tax relief. There is less interest because you have paid off part of your loan. With an endowment mortgage no capital is being repaid so the tax relief remains level throughout the term.

To conclude, if you have spare money to invest and do not want it back for twenty-five years, you might take a full or lower cost with-profits endowment mortgage. If like most people you need and want to spend your spare money now, take a repayment mortgage.

The choice between whether you have a full with-profits or a lower cost policy depends on how much extra you want to save. The premiums on a lower cost policy can be less than half those on a full with-profits policy.

Why mortgage illustrations may mislead

How is it that a repayment mortgage is probably the best bet when mortgage illustrations from insurance companies or brokers always seem to imply that endowment mortgages are so much better? These people do not just assert this – they have figures to prove it. The trouble is that these figures only tell part of the story. In the days when there was little or no inflation they were a reasonable way of illustrating a mortgage over a long period of time – but they no longer are.

First look at the way the salesman's illustration considers the net payments on a repayment mortgage. He does not spell out how the interest payment varies over the term – he quotes an *average* payment. Comparing the average, rather than the *actual* cost of a repayment mortgage with an endowment mortgage, makes the difference between the two appear smaller.

For example the actual cost of a full repayment mortgage in the first year may be £57 a month. Compared with the cost of a full with-profits endowment mortgage of £79 – the endowment is £22 more expensive. But if you use the average cost, which is £66, the endowment seems only £13 more expensive.

The average cost which is used in these mortgage illustrations is the assumed after tax relief cost in every year, added together, and divided by the number of years the mortgage is to run for. However this does not take into account rises in the cost of living. If prices rise by 10% each year for the next ten years (as they have for a long time now) today's £100 payment will be more costly than a payment of £250 in ten years' time.

Averaging all the payments together, however, assumes that

the payments in ten years' time are worth the same as those you make today. We all know that will not be so. But the usual illustrations which purport to show the superiority of an endowment mortgage rely on the fact that the endowment method is cheaper in the later years – in the case of a lower cost endowment perhaps from year twelve or seventeen onwards.[7] However remember that with inflation it is better to save on payments now, rather than later when the saving is lessened by the rise in the cost of living.

Inflation also affects the 'total' cost of the mortgage. With a repayment mortgage the 'total' cost is your payments after tax relief in every year added together. With an endowment the 'total' cost is your after tax interest plus the premiums on the policy added together; also there will be a cash surplus from the maturity value of your with-profits policy after paying off the loan and this is deducted from your total payments to give a net 'total' cost.

However the maturity value of the endowment policy does not arise until year twenty-five when it is paid in 'bad' pounds (i.e. pounds which buy less than today's). Whereas the payments and premiums are made over the years and are paid in 'good' or at least 'better' pounds. All these illustrations which compare profits and costs over long periods into the future should be adjusted for inflation. This is possible with the use of compound interest tables or a financial calculator.

Many academics have seen this point – and it has been made in books and newspaper and magazine articles.[8] Nevertheless the implications seem to have had a much slower effect on the people who prepare these mortgage illustrations. I am afraid the reason is self-evident. It makes endowment mortgages less attractive – and therefore cuts down the possibility of profit for the intermediary or insurance company.

Ending your mortgage early

Many people move house well before the end of their mortgage term. If they have a repayment or option mortgage they just pay off the amount outstanding with the proceeds of the sale and then can make a new choice of what sort of mortgage to have on their new home.

Where you have repaid the mortgage during the first five years or so you may be asked to pay a redemption charge. Sometimes this charge is waived if you give three months' notice or if you take out a new loan from the same society a short while afterwards. Most of the largest societies no longer make an early redemption charge. These include the five largest, the Halifax, Abbey National, Nationwide, Leeds Permanent and Woolwich Equitable.

If you had an endowment mortgage you must decide what to do with the policy. On moving house you are likely to be taking a larger mortgage and the endowment policy will not be large enough to cover the whole loan. If you take a new endowment policy to cover the difference, it will often be more expensive as the cost of life insurance policies increases with age.

You could ask the new lender whether he will allow you to have a part repayment, part endowment mortgage using your existing endowment policy to cover the endowment portion. Some societies will allow the repayment portion to mature at the end of, say, twenty-five years even if the endowment policy only has fifteen years more to run.

With an existing full with-profits policy the lender may be prepared to take into account some or all of the bonuses which have been added to the policy as well as the basic sum insured. This depends on the agreement between your particular society and the insurance company with which you have your policy.

Some lower cost endowment policies now include the option to increase their size when you increase your mortgage. This is not much different from taking out an extra policy except that should your health have deteriorated since you took out the policy, you do not have to pay extra premiums on account of your bad health; but you do have to pay extra on account of your increased age.

If you are short of money, another alternative is to keep your endowment policy going completely separate from the mortgage, borrow extra against its security from the insurance company or your bank and take out a repayment mortgage.

Whatever you do, it is well worth keeping up a with-profits policy – what you get back on maturity is often worth a great deal more than if you surrender (i.e. cash it in early), even taking into account the extra premiums you have paid. But if you have a non-profit policy or a with-profits policy with a poor value company[9] then it might be worthwhile cutting your losses.

NOTES

1 See Appendix 2 for table of monthly repayments at different rates of interest and over different periods of time.
2 *Buying a Home on an Option Mortgage*, Department of Environment.
3 See free leaflet with same title, Department of Environment.
4 Assumes mortgage interest rate 11%, repayable over twenty-five years, tax rate 30%.
5 *Money Which?*; *Money Management*; *Planned Savings*.
6 It is possible to have an option endowment mortgage. However this combination seems pointless. The discussion between repayment and endowment in the rest of this chapter refers exclusively to tax relief mortgages.
7 The actual time depends on the rate of interest and rate of income tax applying. At 15% interest and 30% tax it is nineteen years.
8 For example: Advising on House Purchase', Haberman, S. and Karsten, J., *Accountancy*, January 1977; 'Getting a Mortgage', *Money Which?*, December 1977. The same results apply when mortgages are paid off early. See *House Purchase; the Effects of Moving*, Haberman, S., City University, October 1978 (unpublished). *Daily Mail*, 16 January 1980.
9 See surveys in *Money Which?*; *Money Management*; *The Economist*; *Planned Savings*.

7

Conveyancing and Solicitors

When people talk about the deeds of a house they usually mean the pile of legal documents which prove the ownership of a house. A conveyance is a deed which conveys a house from the vendor (the person selling) to the purchaser.

The legal process

In the UK, other than in Scotland where things are done differently, see p. 83, the purchase of a house is made in two stages. The first stage is up to when contracts are exchanged. This is the most important part. The contract is your written agreement to purchase the property and the vendor's agreement to sell it to you. It describes what is being sold (e.g. the dwelling house known as 32 Hillview Gardens), the price to be paid and any extras or special conditions which have been agreed (e.g. to include carpets, lawn mower, to repair garden fence before leaving). It also gives the date when the deal will be completed – usually four weeks later. The contract includes a lot of standard conditions which describe amongst other things what happens if things go wrong. These standard conditions may be included by a clause referring to them even though they are not usually written into the contract (e.g. National Conditions of Sale Current Edition shall apply to this contract).

There are two identical copies of the contract and solicitors send draft contracts back and forth to each other with suggested amendments until you and the other party are agreed on all the points. If you are being granted a new lease then this is the time to agree all the points and clauses of the lease. If you are buying an existing lease you have to accept the lease as it stands.

When all these details have been hammered out, and also when your solicitor has completed his enquiries and searches (see below), you 'exchange' contracts. That is you sign your copy of the contract and the person you are buying from or selling to signs his copy. Then you exchange copies, the buyer paying a deposit – usually 10% – either to the seller's solicitor or his estate agent.

Exchanging contracts really should be done simultaneously so that you do not end up obliged to sell without the purchaser being obliged to buy and vice-versa. To get round this problem, the purchaser's solicitor sends his contract, signed but undated to the vendor's solicitor, and then (often by telephone) they agree the date to put in to make the transaction valid.

Between exchanging contracts and completion (i.e. the date when you are allowed to move in), your solicitor carries out some more investigations. He 'investigates the title'. This means he checks through the old conveyance going back at least fifteen years to make sure that the person selling actually owns the land. An 'abstract of title' is a summary of old conveyances. If the person selling has owned the house for more than fifteen years then it is only the last conveyance which needs to be looked at. With registered property (see below) the solicitor has no deeds or conveyances to investigate; he merely sends a search form to the Land Registry for its certificate that no further entry has been made since the copy supplied by the vendor's solicitor before the contracts were exchanged.

On completion the balance of the price is exchanged for the deeds (including the transfer document signed by the vendor) and the keys: the purchaser then owns the house. After completion any stamp duty is paid and the transfer, and mortgage, are registered at the Land Registry if applicable.

It often takes two to three months before you sign the contract and another month before completion. However if you are unlucky to get caught in a chain of transactions in which one of the purchasers is delayed in obtaining a mortgage or whose deal falls through, you may end up spending as long as nine months to a year before you finally move into your new home.

Registered and unregistered land

In England and Wales all land is either registered or unregistered. Since 1899 land registration has gradually been made compulsory over different areas of the country. Whether a property is already registered will depend in which area it is situated and how recently it was last sold. It is estimated that 70% of private houses are now within compulsory registration areas – so there is a good chance that the house you are buying is already registered – or will have to be registered after the transaction.

Once a property is registered in someone's name there is a State guarantee of ownership. The deeds and old conveyances can be dispensed with and are replaced by a Land Certificate which is a copy of a register kept at the local branch of the Land Registry.

Enquiries before contract

Before he advises you to sign a contract, the purchaser's solicitor sends the vendor's solicitor a list of questions about the house. Most of these are standard and most solicitors use a printed form with standard questions. Usually the answers are also in a standard form and part of the skill of a seller's solicitor is to conceal anything of importance (which might put somebody off buying) without making any false statements. This may mean the buyer does not get an answer to some questions – and other answers are such that you might as well have been given no reply. If you ask about the state of repair of the house for instance, the answer will almost certainly be something along the lines, 'The purchaser should rely on a survey'.

If there are any points which have not been fully answered and your solicitor thinks that the lack of response may be a clue to something adverse, he will probably seek clarification from the vendor's solicitor. He may also suggest you go and check whether some visible features of the property – like a right of way or a boundary fence – are actually where the deeds say they are. A solicitor rarely inspects a property himself – which is a good reason why you should go back and check that the documents match up with the house.

Local authority searches

This is a form with another set of standard questions which is sent to the local authority by the purchaser's solicitor and the replies obtained prior to signing the contract. Due to the rather ponderous procedure whereby your search has to be passed from department to department within the local authority, this can be a delaying factor in getting the contract exchanged. Your solicitor may get the search form back in a week – or it may take six to eight weeks. If there is any industrial action at the Town Hall you can be quite sure of long delays.

If the local authority searches are expected to be clear, a contract can be signed subject to the searches being okay when they come. Solicitors are reluctant to advise clients to do this just in case something unexpected crops up which may lead to a dispute as to whether the contract should be completed or not.

Where a previous deal has fallen through, it may be possible that the vendor can obtain recent searches from the purchaser who has let him down (he should offer to pay for them) and pass them on to the new purchaser. Replies to searches are usually taken as 'holding good' for two months.

The purpose of the local authority search is to bring to light amongst other things such important facts as whether a motorway is planned to pass through or near the property, or the area is scheduled for slum clearance. The answers you get from local authorities are limited – they will not tell you about road improvements more than so many hundred metres from your boundary for example. And if you are new to an area it would be very wise to make some additional personal enquiries at the Town Hall about local authority plans: reading the local newspapers regularly might also highlight something significant.

Land charges registry search

The land charges registry search paradoxically only applies to unregistered land and the purchaser's solicitor finds out from it whether the vendor is bankrupt or someone has registered a charge (other than a first mortgage) on the property, e.g. a second mortgage which the vendor has not disclosed. Again it is merely a matter of filling in a form and mostly nothing of significance shows up. This type of search is made against the names of the owners of the property (past and present) not against the property itself. The Land Charges Registry for the whole country is at Plymouth.

Other things that solicitors do

The Law Society in its evidence to the Royal Commission on Legal Services[1] was asked to describe in chart form the steps necessary to complete various forms of conveyancing transactions. In the charts provided, a very noticeable feature is the amount of advice and help which solicitors are expected to provide which is not of a legal nature.

For instance solicitors may advise clients on the suitability of a survey (always I hope), may instruct a surveyor for the client and obtain and often interpret the report for their clients; they may advise clients on finance, the mortgage offer and whether or not they should take an endowment mortgage – all strictly non-legal and all matters which the client may or may not be better able to do himself.

A purchaser's solicitor may, at your request, negotiate with the vendor's solicitor over price and the state of repair of the property. He should ensure insurance cover is arranged from the date of the exchange of contracts (if a mortgage is involved the lender will probably do this automatically but will need to know the date of exchange). It is the date of the contract, not completion, when the fire risk passes to the purchaser.

Of course in negotiations over price and so forth your solicitor may merely be acting as a post box for your instructions. Whether or not you think you could do better negotiating direct with the vendor or purchaser is up to you to decide. There is no law that says you have to communicate with the other side through your solicitor – although it is sensible to keep him informed of what you are doing, just so that he does not do something inconsistent with your intentions.

Remember that whenever you have a solicitor acting for you, he should follow your instructions. You may ask for his advice and he may give you advice which you choose to ignore (sometimes at your peril) but if you ignore his advice you have only yourself to blame. On the other hand you may think his advice is completely misguided – and if it is on a non-legal matter like the type of mortgage to take or whether you think the survey report is to be relied on, then do not be afraid to have the courage of your convictions. If he strongly disagrees with you, it may be worth getting a second opinion from someone else.

Choosing a solicitor

If you decide to use a solicitor to represent you and you do not already know one, ask your friends if they can recommend someone. Make sure that the recommendation is based on the solicitor having actually represented them rather than being a casual golf club or bar acquaintance.

Even if recommended, ask the solicitor for an estimate of how much he will charge and compare it with some other estimates. Do not be fobbed off by the sort of answers which two *Daily Mail* readers reported in a survey.[2] 'I asked for an estimate beforehand but was told the fee would be kept as low as possible.' Or from the solicitor who was deeply insulted on being asked for an estimate. 'Do you expect me to hawk my services round like a common pedlar?' he replied and slammed down the telephone.

For every awkward solicitor there are probably ten others ready and willing to give an estimate and with every intention of keeping close to it. If you get a stand-offish response, go elsewhere.

The attitude of the girl who answers the solicitor's telephone may be some guide to the efficiency with which he runs his office. In a small one or two partner firm it is possible that she may do much of the conveyancing herself.

Remember to ask the solicitor whether he is on the panel of the building society where you hope to get your loan. If he is not you will be lumbered with unnecessary extra expense. If you have difficulty finding a solicitor on the building society panel, ask your building society branch manager to recommend at least two so you have a chance to compare estimates (see Chapter 4 under *Solicitors charges*).

Unless you have been recommended someone in particular, I suggest you go for the cheapest – except of course if you know of someone who was not satisfied with the service obtained from him.

Doing your own conveyancing

The normal reason for doing your own conveyancing is to save money. However I would not normally advise a first time buyer to contemplate a do-it-yourself job. With no previous experience of house purchase he is liable to be at a serious disadvantage when dealing with a building society, estate agents, the vendor and the vendor's solicitor. In any case he will still have to pay the fees of a solicitor to act for the building society over the mortgage at a higher rate than would be charged if this solicitor was also acting for him. And he will not be saving any fees on a sale. So his scope for cutting costs is limited. Advice on how to keep a solicitor's conveyancing charges down is given in Chapter 4.

For someone who has experience of buying a house previously, doing the conveyance yourself can be a worthwhile way of saving money; especially if you are selling a house at the same time – you save both sets of legal fees. Some people think you should do your own conveyancing not only to save money but because you are likely to do a more thorough job. This would seem an unusual point of view – to insist that a layman can do a better job than the expert. But it is argued very convincingly by its chief advocate Michael Joseph in his book *The Conveyancing Fraud.*

Michael Joesph is a solicitor himself and spent fifteen years practising in conveyancing before he saw the light. His main thesis is that most conveyancing as practised by solicitors has developed into a ritual: often the steps in the transactions are not performed by solicitors but by their clerks (who may or may not be 'qualified' as members of the Institute of Legal Executives), and many if not all the really important points are left to chance. He reckons that what the layman lacks in experience he can make up in enthusiasm and by taking extra care: thoroughly inspecting the property himself and calling personally at the local authority instead of relying on standard forms of enquiry – with often meaningless or evasive answers to far too general questions.

Michael Joesph claims that conveyancing is neither complicated nor difficult. He say anyone capable of getting his own passport or road tax licence is capable not only of doing his own conveyancing but doing a far better job than a professional. But only you can judge whether you have the confidence and patience to do it yourself.

Buying a house takes time. If you are selling as well it takes even longer. You should not normally sign a contract to buy a new house until you are ready to sign a contract to sell your existing one. If you do, you may be left owning two houses – but with only enough money to pay for one. The same thing may happen to the chap you are buying from. If somewhere along the line someone is unable to get fixed up with a mortgage, many other people's purchases and sales can be held up. This is called a mortgage-chain. One reason for using a solicitor is that he can sometimes use his influence to find a mortgage for someone further down the chain and thus get all the transactions rolling again.

My own view is that if you are contemplating doing your own

conveyancing, then you should remember that it is far easier on a sale. After all the only really important thing for you to ensure is that you have the money at the end of the transaction – it is up to the purchaser to sort out any complications. On a purchase, if you have a mortgage, you will have to pay the building society's solicitor and he is likely to be checking that you have done the right things (but do not rely on it); your best safeguard is that he cannot protect the building society's mortgage unless he also protects you. Buying registered land means you will not have to draft a conveyance – although an update of the last one may not be that difficult to work out.

However there are a few instances where I would definitely advise against doing your own conveyancing: when you are buying a newly built house, when you are being granted a new lease or when you are buying a hitherto unregistered house in what is now a compulsory registration area. In the first two cases snags on which you will require legal advice are likely to occur – and you will probably have to make the first registration which is usually more work than the registration of a transfer; in the latter case you definitely will have to make the first registration. In any event, people who do not have easy access to a typewriter and a photocopying machine will find do-it-yourself conveyancing very tedious. It is obviously essential, for example, to keep a copy of all your correspondence and of the documents.

There are two books I would recommend for someone contemplating do-it-yourself conveyancing: Michael Joseph's *The Conveyancing Fraud*, and for registered freehold property only *The Legal Side of Buying a House* published by the Consumers, Association. Both are available through bookshops or direct from the publisher.[3] If you want to know more about conveyancing, even if you do not want to do it yourself, the books I have mentioned are still worth reading.

Cut price conveyancing organisations

There are a number of organisations which offer conveyancing services to the public. They are usually run by people who used to work in solicitors' offices as 'legal executives' or 'managing clerks' and who may be as experienced in the practical side of conveyancing as any solicitor. Their advantage is that they can be a lot cheaper than solicitors – often half price or even less.

The Law Society sets out the reasons why you should not go to a cut price conveyancing organisation in a pamphlet.[4] 'There are very few services that cannot be provided – by unqualified people – at a lower price than what is charged by those who do have a professional qualification. Those for whom price is the *only* consideration are the natural prey of the unqualified conveyancer,' it says.

The pamphlet also lists a number of benefits of retaining solicitors which it says do not apply to unqualified organisations. The most important of these in my opinion are that a solicitor must observe strict rules about keeping your money separate from his, he is covered by professional negligence insurance and the Law Society compensation fund (in case he runs off with your deposit) and he must never act for two people whose interests may conflict.

It would therefore be wise to enquire of a cut price conveyancing organisation whether they are covered by professional indemnity insurance, for how much (£100,000 at least) and whether they are fidelity bonded (i.e. there is an insurance policy which will pay you if they run off with your money). Also ask for their most recent report and accounts which should give you an idea of their scale of operations.

It might also be wise not to let any of your money actually be held by the conveyancing organisation. This may involve, if they act for the vendor, opening a special joint bank account to hold the deposit – and having to attend the completion personally to hand over or receive the purchase money.

Title insurance

A couple of cut price conveyancing organisations offer Title Insurance as part of their service. This guarantees you against the insured loss if there should turn out to be a defect in your owner-ship and could help with the legal costs of a boundary dispute for instance. It pays you compensation if you lose the case as well. Solicitors consider this insurance cover to be a gimmick and unnecessary and there seem to be very few claims. But if it costs you no extra, you might as well have it.

Scotland

One of the first things you will notice when contemplating buying a house in Scotland is that solicitors also act as estate agents. They are even allowed to call themselves 'Solicitor and Estate Agent'. As well as the normal methods used for buying and selling property in the rest of the UK (i.e. newspaper adverts, For Sale boards and circulars to interested parties) there are also Solicitors Property Centres.

At a Solicitors Property Centre you will find details of much of the local heritable property (the name Scottish lawyers use to describe property of the bricks and mortar variety). This is likely to provide a similar service to that of a rather large display in an estate agent's window. The difference is that it will have property on offer from all the solicitors in the area so if there is no estate agent nearby you need go no further – except perhaps to look over the local newspaper for someone selling privately.

Only solicitors can advertise properties through Solicitors Property Centres although, of course, anyone can buy through them. Commission is charged by a solicitor for selling a house in addition to his conveyancing fee. The purchaser does not have to pay this extra fee – only the vendor. The maximum commission for a sale which a solicitor can charge is $1\frac{1}{2}\%$ of the price, but if he also does your conveyancing he should generally charge less than this; how much less depends on how much work he put into selling it. He can also add the cost of advertising.

Charges for conveyancing are on a scale recommended by the Law Society of Scotland. A solicitor can also charge extra for postage and telephone calls. Scales of commissions for selling and fees for conveyancing and dealing with the mortgage are given in a leaflet.[5] To be quite sure of what you can expect to pay, always ask for a quotation or estimate as you would elsewhere in the UK.

Dealing with offers

The major difference between English and Scottish land law is that in Scotland there is no such thing as an offer 'subject to contract'.[6] Any written offer you make can be binding on you – provided the other party chooses to accept it in writing. And the bargain can be concluded within twenty-four hours.

Although sales contracts, drafted and redrafted by the parties, are known in Scotland (as they are in the rest of the UK), they are uncommon and confined to complex business transactions.

Private house purchase is usually handled by a system known as 'missives of sale'. A missive of sale is a written offer to buy a house in Scotland; it is binding on the person making it but not until the seller accepts it.

Before you send the missive you need to have your survey (and the building society valuation) made. The local authority enquiries are made by the vendor's solicitor – not by the purchaser's solicitor as elsewhere in the UK – so there will be no delay waiting for those.

Where there are several people competing for the same house, this is obviously a boom for local surveyors. Unfortunately there is little alternative as rarely will a seller agree to make a contract subject to a survey or the purchaser obtaining a mortgage. If a competing offer is accepted you have wasted the cost of your structural survey and building society valuation (which you have to pay for as you do elsewhere in the UK whether or not you take the loan). If you can find out (from the vendor) which surveyor has surveyed the property for another would-be purchaser, you might get him to do it again for you at a reduced fee.

Preparing the missive is quite a skilled job. For instance the seller may set a time limit by which he wants offers submitted. This will usually be the case where there is a lot of competition for the house. He will obviously want to sell to the highest bidder – which can be a bit perplexing at times of rapid house price inflation. If you are advised by your surveyor and solicitor that a house is worth £18,000 and to put in an offer of £19,000 – it can be very disappointing if it goes to someone who offered £22,000 when you were ready to pay that amount if necessary. On the other hand had you offered £23,000 you could remain blissfully ignorant that the next highest offer was only £17,500. Deciding on the price to offer when there are competing bidders is the most difficult part of the procedure in Scotland. The vendor's solicitor is not allowed to disclose what offers he has received – so all but one are bound to be disappointed. A local solicitor is usually the best source of advice on how much to offer.

Just as the seller may set a time limit by which he wants his offers in, you may often decide to put a time limit after which your offer lapses. If the property has been difficult to sell and you are making a low offer then the time limit might be short to encourage acceptance rather than for the seller to hang on to see if a better offer will turn up. A seller may of course not accept your offer simply because he is waiting for his offer to purchase another house to be accepted. The Scottish system of binding missives means that the transaction is generally quicker than in England and Wales.

As well as the price offered and a description of the property the missive will contain the 'date of entry' which is when you have to pay up and can move in. Convenient dates for both parties will usually have been discussed verbally – and of course an alternative date can always be agreed mutually.

Bridging loans seem to be looked upon more favourably by Scottish solicitors than their English counterparts. This may be because the only way to secure a house is to enter into a binding contract – which you may have to do before you sell your old home.

There is no preliminary 10% deposit – the whole price is paid on 'settlement', the Scottish equivalent of 'completion'. Sometimes the price is paid in instalments – although according to the Law Society of Scotland a more satisfactory system is to treat the unpaid balance as a mortgage by the seller.[7]

Conveyancing

All property in Scotland is recorded in the Sasine Register, a property register established in 1617 and kept at Edinburgh. The Sasine Register also records mortgages and some other information and is open to public inspection. It differs from the English system of registered property because an entry in the Sasine Register does not guarantee that the deed registered there is valid (i.e. that the person who purports to own the property actually does so). It has been proposed to introduce Land Registration along the lines of the English system but it will be many years before this comes fully into effect.

Whereas in England for unregistered land a solicitor must look back at the title for fifteen years, in Scotland the period is ten years. Otherwise conveyancing is carried out by a system of deeds rather like the transfer of unregistered property in England and Wales. You will find the Scots have their own legal jargon which is no easier (or more difficult) to understand than English legal jargon.

I know of no book on do–it–yourself conveyancing in Scotland. It would therefore be unwise to attempt a transaction on this basis without a guide of what to do.

Northern Ireland

The system of property transfer in Northern Ireland is broadly similar to that in England and Wales although contracts are often signed speedily subject to a buyer obtaining a mortgage within a specified period and local authority enquiries being made and found satisfactory. A deposit of 10% is paid on exchange of contracts and is usually held by the seller's solicitor. It is returnable if the conditions of the contract are not met.

The organisation for solicitors in Northern Ireland is the Incorporated Law Society of Northern Ireland. You may find it more difficult to do your own conveyancing as the do–it–yourself guides do not explain the differences between English and Northern Ireland practices.

Forms of ownership

Where you are buying a property jointly (with your husband or wife for example), there are two legal ways in which a property may be held. These are 'joint tenancy' and 'tenancy in common'.

Provided both owners remain living in the house there is no practical difference. With a joint tenancy if the husband dies first, say, the house automatically passes to his wife, irrespective of what he puts in his will. This is not the case with a tenancy in common where the husband's share would become part of his estate and pass according to the provisions of his will.

For many years solicitors automatically made joint purchases by a husband and wife into joint tenancies. This was because there was often an Estate Duty advantage by doing so. Nowadays since the advent of Capital Transfer Tax, there is no advantage – and there could be an advantage in having a tenancy in common.

A joint tenancy can be severed by either party giving notice to the other. In such a case the ownership becomes a tenancy in common. If you particularly want to leave your half of the house to someone other than the person who owns the other half – then you should ensure that you have a tenancy in common. A solicitor is the best person to go for advice on this matter.

NOTES

1 Memorandum No. 3: Replies by the Council of the Law Society to the request for evidence from the Law Society by the Royal Commission, 1977.
2 *Daily Mail*, 14 September 1977.
3 For addresses see Appendix 3.
4 *Buying and Selling Your Home: Questions and Answers about Conveyancing*, Law Society.
5 *Buying or Selling a House*, Law Society of Scotland. For address see Appendix 3.
6 See also *Transfer of Land 'Subject to Contract'*, Law Commission Working Paper, HMSO, 1973.
7 Replies by the Law Society of Scotland to the Royal Commission on Legal Services in Scotland, Volume 1, October 1977.

8

Household Insurance

Your home is likely to be the most valuable asset you ever own. It is therefore essential that it is insured. Most likely you have also spent your remaining savings on furnishing it as nicely as possible so the same should surely apply to the contents.

Having pronounced in favour of insurance, you should be under no illusion that insurance can compensate you for every piece of bad luck which befalls you. In fact the cynical would say that many an insurance policy seems to exclude all but the most rare occurrences.

Household insurance policies do not cover everything. You insure against certain named 'perils' like fire, flood and theft. If you incur a loss or damage to your property as a result of these perils the insurance company pays out provided you have kept your insurance cover up to the right amount.

With items which depreciate in value, in the past you were never paid enough to replace the stolen or destroyed items as new. Your claim value was worked out according to the principle of 'indemnity'. Such a claim was calculated by deducting an appropriate proportion from the current replacement cost. One way of assessing this is to work out the useful life of an item; for instance if it were fifteen years for a three piece suite, they might knock off one-third from the replacement cost for a five-year-old suite.

Rather than haggling with an insurance company over a claim, it is better to put all your household insurance on a 'new-for-old' basis. You pay higher premiums but there should be no dispute about replacement costs – it will be the cost of replacement by a new item (except usually for clothing and bed linen).

Household insurance policies are usually divided into two parts – buildings and contents. Insurance companies issue package policies containing both, but many people insure their buildings through one company and their contents through another.

Buildings insurance

People buying a home with a mortgage are usually obliged to insure the buildings with an insurance company chosen by the lender. Building societies now give you a choice of three companies – a fairly meaningless choice as the cost and conditions are likely to be identical. But if your house is liable to a higher than average premium – say four to eight times for a thatched cottage – it is worth shopping around yourself and trying to persuade the building society to use a cheaper company.

In the case of a flat there is usually one buildings insurance policy for the whole block. Each tenant pays his share of the premium but normally has no say in the choice of insurance company – the landlord is obliged, under the terms of the lease, to make sure that the insurance is adequate.

Inclusions and exclusions

The policy normally covers damage caused by fire, earthquake, lightning, explosion, storm, flood, water escaping from pipes or tanks, impact of aircraft, rail and road vehicles or animals, falling trees, theft or attempted theft, breakage of aerials, oil leaking from central heating installations, riot or malicious damage (but not in Northern Ireland) and subsidence land-slip.

In the case of subsidence or landslip you normally have to pay the first 3% of the total rebuilding cost of your house or the first £250 whichever is the higher. For a £25,000 house this means you pay the first £750 of any subsidence or landslip claim. In the case of escaping water, impact by a vehicle driven by you or a member of your family living with you, or damage as a result of riot, malicious damage or falling trees, the first £15 is often not covered. You can usually pay an extra premium to have this £15 'excess' deleted. However it is not really worthwhile deleting such small excesses. The subsidence excess cannot be deleted.

If the damage is so bad you have to live elsewhere until it is repaired, then the insurance will often pay the cost of alternative accommodation up to a maximum of 10% of what the building is insured for.

In addition to the structure a buildings policy covers interior decorations, built-in furniture, sanitary fittings, plumbing and central heating, greenhouses, toolsheds, fences and garden walls, drives, gates and even swimming pools. Breakage of glass, in windows or doors and bathroom fittings, may also be covered – whatever the cause of damage.

Common exclusions are frost damage, storm or flood damage to gates and fences, escaping water damage if the house is left partially furnished or unfurnished for more than thirty days, and damage caused by war, civil war, rebellion or revolution.

Apart from the exclusions in the policy, insurance companies may refuse to pay out on a claim for some other reason – when what they call a 'material fact' has not been disclosed by you. Insurance companies have agreed with the Government[1] that they should ask you direct questions about material facts (and if they do not, you should disclose them).

These material facts include whether the house is used for a business (even part time), whether you leave the home unattended regularly during the daytime, whether you take lodgers, whether it is in an area subject to flood, subsidence or landslip, whether it is in good repair, whether in the past three years there has been an occurrence of any of the risks which are to be insured, whether the house is built of material other than brick, stone or concrete, and roofed with anything apart from tiles, metal, asphalt or concrete and whether it is a holiday home or otherwise left empty for long periods. If any of these apply, you can expect to pay higher premiums or have your cover restricted.

How much to insure for

What you pay for your house is not necessarily how much you should insure it for. When you buy with a building society mortgage, the building society valuer should make an insurance valuation which is what the building society will insure it for. Nowadays most building societies insist on policies where the amount insured and premiums are linked to an index of building costs. This way you ensure that the insurance value does not fall behind because of inflation. If your policy is not index-linked, you should update the insured value every year.

The British Insurance Association now has a guide to building costs which it intends to revise at suitable intervals. For more details you can get a free leaflet;[2] insurance companies also have their own leaflets and help is given in *Money Which?* magazine. Rebuilding costs depend on the size of the house; when it was built; whether it is a 'semi', detached, terraced or a bungalow; and how much rebuilding costs are in the region in which it is situated. For details of how this varies by region see Table 8.

The cost of a buildings policy is £12.50 to £15 for each £10,000 worth of insurance. If your house is of non-standard construction you can pay from half as much again to eight times more.

Contents insurance

'Contents' comprise furniture, household goods and appliances (e.g. washing machine, cooker, fridge, television, Hi-fi), clothing, moveable fixtures and fittings, furnishings (like carpets and curtains), food, drink; and valuables such as jewellery and money up to specified limits. Internal decorations come under the buildings policy – but may be covered under the contents in certain cases, e.g. a leasehold flat.

Single items are usually limited to, say, 5% of the total value you are insured for – unless you specify them to the insurance company. And usually not more than a third of the value must consist of valuables – defined as jewellery, gold and silver, furs

Table 8 Examples of house prices compared with insurance values

	Market price £	Estimated insured value £
Non basement		
2 bedroom terrace		
pre 1920		
Nottingham	6 825	24 168
Cardiff	8 675	25 243
Brighton	14 250	26 854
Semi-detached		
3 bedroom 1930s		
Leeds	13 725	27 759
Cambridge	18 750	26 578
Edinburgh	26 125	29 531
Finchley (London)	35 000	32 484
Detached		
4 bedroom – modern		
Norwich	29 975	46 967
Manchester	39 000	49 650
Kingston	85 000	59 044

Source: Prices from National Association of Estate Agents Survey December 1978. Estimated insured values based on British Insurance Association recommended figures at December 1978. By mid-1980 prices were up an estimated 40%; building costs up an estimated 30%.

and so on. Theft is usually excluded when the home is sublet, let or lent unless there is evidence of forcible entry.

The insured 'perils' are the same as under the buildings policy but if you are insured with a different company for buildings than for contents – you may have slightly different cover.

All risks cover

A contents policy does not usually cover your contents outside your house (sometimes outside your garden) except when you are moving house. Nor does it usually cover accidental damage except to specific items – an owned or rented television set is the main example.

Some modern contents policies offer cover for accidental damage caused by your family's own clumsiness. While you may be able to claim for damage caused by burning a hole through a new sofa with a cigarette (because fire is a hazard against which you are insured), you will not be able to claim if you break the family Chinese vase collection unless your contents policy is of the 'all risks' variety. Usually the first £5 or so is excluded from these policies and there are exceptions for wear and tear, vermin, mildew and mechanical breakdown. The snag is that the cost is about double.

Quite separate from 'all risks' on the contents are specific all risks extensions to a traditional contents policy for single valuable items. A valuable engagement ring, camera or fur which is frequently taken out of the house will need to be specified and and an extra premium paid. The rate for this sort of all risks insurance varies very widely but you can expect to pay from four to ten times the premium for the same amount of cover as for your household contents. You can also get extensions for the contents of a freezer and your personal effects outside the home.

Money

Money (including postage stamps, postal orders and season tickets) is covered under an ordinary contents policy but there is generally a £100 limit on a claim. Nor will the company pay for theft unless there is evidence of a forcible and violet entry. Should someone walk through the open front door and pinch your handbag, the bag would be covered but not the money in it. However for an extra premium you can also insure money outside the house up to £200 which would cover you for a walk-in theft.

New-for-old

In the event of a claim on a contents policy, you are likely to be much more satisfied if you have a 'new-for-old' or 'replacement-as-new' policy. This means that you are given the money to buy a new item even though the one destroyed or damaged beyond repair has depreciated in value since you bought it. But wear and tear on clothing and linen is still taken into account. The alternative is an 'indemnity' policy where wear and tear is taken into account on all items.

Some companies issue hybrid policies which are new-for-old during the first three or five years of the life of a large item (e.g. carpets, furniture) and indemnity thereafter; as well as indemnity for everything else.

I would strongly recommend a new-for-old policy. Having a new-for-old policy does mean that you should have a higher insured value than if you had an indemnity policy. But it is quite simple to work out – you just go round the shops totting up the prices of buying everything you have brand new. The easiest way is to make a list room by room.[3]

The cost of contents and all risks cover

Whilst buildings insurance often costs £12.50 to £15 for each £10,000 of insurance anywhere in the country, the cost of contents cover varies widely and is related to the varying in-cidence of theft in different parts of the country – and even different areas in the same town.

The cheapest will be around £25 for each £10,000 of insurance – although of course your contents are unlikely to be as valuable as your home so the actual premium you pay may be less.

Contents insurance is particularly expensive in all London postal districts (especially North-West London and the West End), and the nearby areas of Edgware, Stanmore and Harrow. The next most expensive areas are the rest of Greater London, Liverpool and Glasgow. If you have been with the same company for a long time they may not have increased your rate to what they would charge a newcomer.

All risks insurance for individual items outside the house comes even more expensive. The premium would be from 1 to 3%, say £10 to £30 a year for a £1,000 fur coat.

If you live in one of the areas I have mentioned above it is worth getting quotes from more than one insurance company as not all have the same rates for the same areas. You may have to pay higher rates if you live in a flat. Installing new locks might help to keep your premium down or may even be required before a company will accept you in a high risk area.

New policies are often index-linked – so the insured value and premiums are automatically increased. If you buy extra furniture, make sure you increase your insurance cover.

Legal liability

This is usually included with both buildings and contents policies. It covers you for your liability as a houseowner (buildings) or as an occupier (contents) if you are sued, for example, for accidents to visitors to your home for which you are legally responsible. There is normally a limit of £250,000 on such claims.

Legal expenses insurance

This is a completely separate policy from your other household insurance policies and has not really caught on yet. As far as I know only one insurer offers it.[4]

A legal expenses insurance policy covers your legal costs if you get involved in a legal action. And if you lose it pays any costs awarded against you (but not damages).

Although there may be some serious exclusions (e.g. no claims against builders you have employed or against insurance companies) this can be a very helpful form of insurance for someone who at some time in the future is likely to get into a dispute and need legal advice which he may not be able to afford. The policy costs from £20 to £30 a year and there is a maximum limit on your claim of from £10,000 to £15,000.

The sort of disputes these policies cover are those with traders such as shopkeepers, cleaners, garages and travel agents. And also disputes with neighbours, employers, landlords and public authorities.

NOTES

1 *Statement of Insurance Practice*, British Insurance Association 1977.
2 *A Guide to Buildings Insurance for the Homeowner*, British Insurance Association.
3 See also the free leaflet *A Guide to Home Contents Insurance*, British Insurance Association.
4 DAS Legal Expenses Insurance Co. Ltd. Phoenix Assurance Ltd. offers the same policy as an addition to its house policies.

9

Living in Your Home

Having overcome all the hurdles of dealing with estate agents, building societies, surveyors, solicitors, insurance companies and well meaning relatives – all of whom seem to have been sent to try you – you may now be ready to live happily ever after in your new home. And most people do.

However a major difference between an owner-occupier and a tenant is that an owner-occupier must make his own decisions. He cannot leave everything to the landlord – and he has no one but himself (or his wife) to blame if things do not go as planned. So this chapter is aimed at giving you a few hints on how to live happily in your home.

Rates and rateable value

Probably the first bill to come in will be the rates. This is a property tax collected by the local council. You may not have had to pay rates as a tenant – they may have been included in your rent.

Rates are based on the rateable value of your home. The rateable value is supposed to represent the rent at which your home could be let to a tenant after deduction of a fixed scale for maintenance. Rateable values are revalued at general valuations which tend to take place at long intervals – every five or ten years. So in practice the rateable value is no more than an arbitrary value put on your home.

In between valuations your rateable value may be increased if you make significant improvements to your home (e.g. an extension) and the council gets to know. Building a garage would also raise your rateable value. But since 1974 if you put in central heating you do not have the rateable value raised until the next revaluation.

This has resulted in an unfair situation where, for example, two identical houses, located side by side and both with central heating, have different rateable values: one having installed central heating before 1974 and the other after. An example in Barnes shows one house at a rateable value of £584 and the one next door £547.[1]

You can appeal against your rateable value between general revaluations – for instance if your amenities are affected by a kennels opening up next door or a school or factory being built next to your back garden.[2]

People who appeal against their rates need to have a lot of time on their hands. You are likely to achieve a small reduction (assuming you succeed which you may not) in relation to the amount of work and effort put in. I do not recommend it.

If you do succeed in getting the rateable value permanently reduced you have made an investment for the future (provided you do not move away) as the rates you pay are based on a certain number of pence for each pound of rateable value. For example if the rate in the pound is 90p and your rateable value £100, your rates are £90. The rate, which is fixed each year by your local council, tends to rise every year so, if you manage to have the rateable value reduced, each year you will have saved more money.

Paying the rates

You pay the rates to the Finance Department of your local council. The bill often comes in two instalments – in April and

October. You can either pay it by the time stated on the demand or you have the right to pay by ten or more equal instalments; it is most convenient to arrange a standing order at your bank for these. A few councils give you a discount, say 2½% off, if you pay the whole lot in advance. This saving is not really worth while and paying by instalments is what most people do. You can be prosecuted and imprisoned for not paying the rates.

Rate rebates

There are also rate rebates whereby you may be able to get a reduction or rebate on your rates if your income is low in relation to the rates you pay. There is no upper limit on incomes but there is on rateable values; a rebate is not payable on houses with rateable values over £1,500 in Greater London or over £750 elsewhere.

This does mean that in the highest rateable value areas, especially in Greater London, quite well off people can get rate rebates. In theory people with incomes up to £23,000 a year might sometimes be eligible for a rate rebate. This is not obvious because the leaflet[3] on rate rebates only gives examples for low incomes and low amounts of rates paid.

The rebates are higher for families with children and one parent families; they are lower if your children are in regular employment. There is also a special extra rate rebate for severely disabled people.

Water, gas, electricity, fuel, telephone

Water rates now cover the cost of sewage disposal as well as the provision of water. In the past the sewage part was collected as part of the general rate – and the water part separately in two instalments. Water authorities aim to collect the whole amount themselves but at the time of writing there is no national scheme for paying water rates by more than two instalments. This can be expected to be introduced as the level of water rates rises. You cannot get a rate rebate on the water rate.

Gas and electricity bills are sent quarterly and depending on your method of heating, the winter ones are likely to be much heavier than the summer ones. All gas and electricity boards give you the chance to pay monthly at no extra charge. They use your last year's bills to estimate what next year's will be and divide by twelve to get the monthly payment. At the end of the year you make an adjustment for what you have under or overpaid. Oil and coal bills can often be spread out in monthly payments – but you may get a discount by paying all at once.

Telephone bills come quarterly and the Post Office says it is studying the possibility of introducing an instalment scheme.

Other bills

Other expenditure is likely to be less readily spread. Life insurance premiums can usually be paid monthly rather than annually. Some companies let you pay car insurance in five or six instalments at no extra cost. You can pay your building insurance to the building society by adding one twelfth of the annual premium to your monthly mortgage payments. And the same applies to the contents insurance if you have insured through the building society. Season tickets can sometimes be financed by interest free loans from your employer – ask if he has a scheme. A ground rent and service charge on a flat might be spread to quarterly payments instead of half yearly.

If there are still too many lump sum bills, you could ask your bank if it runs a budget account. But you have to pay a charge and interest for such a facility, unlike most of the methods described above which are free.

Service charges

If you own a flat your lease is likely to provide that the cost of common services is shared between all the tenants. So in addition to your ground rent you get a bill for your share of cleaning the communal halls, maintaining any garden and for any repairs and decorations which are carried out.

Normally the ground landlord or his agents make an estimate of the expenditure in advance and you make payments of an 'advance service charge' towards the cost. Once a year you should be sent audited accounts or receipts showing the total expenditure, and you then have to pay any extra (there never seems to be a refund although there could be).

Large blocks of flats may have a sinking fund to provide for the cost of future large-scale works. This means the money is saved up for three or four years so as to lessen the amount you have to pay when the work is carried out. Unfortunately sinking funds do not work well when inflation is high as they cannot do much to cut the eventual bill.

When expenditure of over £500 is proposed on a single item a landlord must obtain two estimates and let the tenants have the opportunity of seeing and commenting on them at least a month in advance.[4] The freehold of some blocks of flats is owned by a management company which in turn is owned by the residents themselves. So in practice it is the residents' association which is the landlord. Even where this is not so, a well run residents' association, especially in a large block, can negotiate with the landlord's agents and make life for the residents happier.[5]

Heating

One of the most expensive costs of running a home is heating. In this era of so-called energy shortage, saving fuel is now what the government wants everyone to do.

Which? magazine makes periodic surveys of the costs of different forms of heating.

Insulating the loft and lagging your hot water tank are the cheapest ways of saving on heating costs. Details of this and other methods can be found in leaflets published by the Department of Energy,[6] and also in a Department of Environment leaflet.[7] And there is yet another leaflet on heating controls.[7] You can even get a grant from your local council to insulate a loft, hot and cold water tanks and pipes for the first time.[8]

Double glazing, which is expensive, is not recommended as a method of insulating a home against heat loss although it may be useful against noise. Cavity wall insulation, also expensive, may be worth having if your house is of suitable construction. There are a number of trade associations which can give advice on these matters such as the Glass and Glazing Federation and the National Cavity Insulation Association.[9]

If you have not already got central heating, you may think it well worth while to install it. At the time of writing, gas is the cheapest fuel with which to operate central heating and oil the most expensive. However before North Sea Gas and the Middle East oil crisis the opposite was true.

Gas is more convenient in that there is rarely a shortage of supplies (e.g. through a tanker drivers' strike) and you do not need space for a storage tank. However in some country areas gas may not be available. A source of information on this is the Heating and Ventilation Contractors' Association and for gas installers there is CORGI.[10]

Alternatively you might consider solid fuel although this will have to be a special smokeless type – no log fires – if you are in a smokeless zone. Your solicitor's local authority enquiries will give the answer to that. For more details there is a leaflet.[11]

Maintaining your home

Decorations

You will probably want to decorate your new home inside as soon as you move in. And you will probably want to do it yourself. An extremely useful book is the Reader's Digest *Complete Do It Yourself Manual* which not only tells you how to paint, hang wallpaper and put up tiles but also all about almost any household repair or improvement you are likely to want to carry out yourself.

Inside decorations can last quite a long time – so if you do not expect to stay in the same house for more than seven years or so, you will not have to bother to redecorate once you have done it initially. Outside decorations, however, have to be done more frequently – every four years is the usual interval. If you leave it for five years the paint is likely to be peeling off the window frames. You might want to do it every three years if your house is particularly exposed to harsh weather conditions.

If you are making any structural alterations, e.g. rewiring, central heating, or replacing the bathroom, it is obviously sensible to try and time this to take place shortly before you are due to have decorations done. Otherwise you will have to spend extra time touching up the inevitable damage to decorations caused by such installations.

Should you decide to have the decorations done for you – either inside or out – you should ask at least two, preferably three, decorators to give you a quote. Specify in detail what you want done, e.g. two coats of oil paint, garage doors to be stripped to wood, inside of bedroom fitted cupboards included in painting. You could even list a specification, perhaps amending it in the light of a decorator's comments and suggestions as he looks round the house.

Large firms and some small ones will give you a written quote. One-man-bands usually do not. Occasionally you get someone calling who is only acting as an agent for other contractors and will not be doing or superivising the work himself. With a small firm it is always worth asking whether the man you see will be doing or supervising the work.

The quotes you get can often vary enormously. One year I got three contractors to estimate for painting the outside of my house. The quotes were £200, £450 and £600, and with the £600 quote I was to supply my own paint. I chose the cheapest and had a quick but not particularly thorough job done; but it lasted three years.

With smaller contractors one way of keeping the price down, especially where there is a lot of painting, is to get a quote including materials – and then ask how much less it would be if you supplied your own. My experience has been that painters often vastly overestimate the amount of paint needed. They often buy from a trade supplier who may charge more than what you might pay at a do-it-yourself cash and carry. In another instance I was quoted ten gallons of paint at a cost of £9 a gallon. In the end he used six gallons which I bought for £6 a gallon.

Plumbers, electricians, carpenters, roof repairs

Decorating is a relatively unskilled but time consuming job carried out at lengthy intervals. However if something goes wrong with the plumbing or you want an alteration made to the position of a power point, or you want to have a fitted cupboard made or the roof starts to leak, your choice of contractor is more difficult. Taking the cheapest will rarely be the best alternative.

By their nature, poorly done decorations show up and can usually be remedied easily; if a poorly painted window starts peeling, it does not take much to touch it up on a Sunday morning. This is not the case with other sorts of poor workmanship. If a pipe starts leaking as a result of a plumber doing a bad job you have to get him (or another plumber) back immediately to remedy the damage.

So go on recommendation first and price second for such jobs. Of course if you have no recommendation then you will have to get quotes from more than one contractor, except, of course, in cases of emergency. Nevertheless even in an emergency or if you are only considering one man, always ask for an estimate of the cost unless the job is only a small one and you are pretty sure of his general level of charges from a previous job.[12]

Local newspapers are often a source of advertisements for tradesmen. Often good tradesmen are in such demand that you have to wait a very long time for them to come and do the job. There are registration schemes for gas and electrical installers and you can get a list of local registered tradesmen.[13] Installations are best done by people registered with the respective councils.

Noise

You may live in the idyllic countryside but you are more likely to live in a town or suburb. The best way of avoiding noise is not to buy a home affected by it. But the noise may arrive after you move in – or you did not know about it. Information on what to do about noise and how in some circumstances you can get insulation grants are given in two leaflets.[14]

Disputes with neighbours

Disputes with neighbours can make life very difficult – and the fact that you may meet almost daily makes such a dispute one of the most bitter.

Boundaries are the most common cause of a serious dispute. One neighbour's building a fence or wall only a foot (and sometimes less) on the wrong side of a boundary can start all manner of fuss.

Trees are probably the next most common cause. If you own the tree and it causes you damage, you promptly cut it down. But if it is your neighbour who complains of the tree casting shadows over his patio, choking his drains with leaves, breaking his plants with falling branches or undermining his foundations with its roots, it is amazing how essential you may feel the tree is to the leafy environment of the street! You might even get the council to put a preservation order on it.

Other causes of annoyance are children and animals. Large dogs can terrify small children; and medium sized children can terrify elderly widows – often not by what they do but what the neighbour thinks they may do. Disputes over shared driveways, rights of way and even the positioning of garden lights have been known.

There is rarely a satisfactory solution once a dispute gets going until one or other of the neighbours moves away. Arguing over the fence usually makes things worse and getting a solicitor to obtain an injunction against a neighbour to stop his doing something is rarely worth the trouble or expense.

The best approach is undoubtedly a good neighbour policy. Whenever you see your neighbours, exchange a cheery word, pat their dog, comment (favourably) on their children, offer them the occasional plant from the garden. And sometimes do them a small favour. If you have been looking after next door's dog for a week while they are on holiday and you reverse your car straight through their garden wall ruining their favourite flower bed, you are likely to be able to weather the storm far better than if you had never done them a favour. Incidentally that example is a true one – though I hasten to add I was neither car driver nor dog owner.

Lend your step ladder. Look after a spare set of keys. Invite your neighbours in for tea or a drink at Christmas. These are all ways of building up neighbourliness which will lessen the impact of a dispute if it subsequently occurs.

If you fall into dispute and do not want a fight, then the best thing to do is to give in or move elsewhere. If you do not mind a fight you would cut the costs if you had legal expenses insurance (see p. 95).

Securing your home

Professional burglars will probably boast that they can get into any home if they put their minds to it. But the more difficult you make it for them, the less likely they are to try. You should also remember that not all thieves are so expert. An increasing number of children are involved in domestic break-ins and some may be put off by the simplest precautions. Surprisingly enough it is still mainly a matter of locks and bolts. Make sure that all the outside doors to your home have mortice locks on them – and that when you go out, even for ten minutes, you lock them. You may be surprised how little time a thief needs to stay in your home. There is no point in locking inside doors; burglars are then likely to smash them causing you even more aggravation. Closing inside doors unlocked is a useful fire precaution, however.

You can get free advice on what type of locks – and whether

you need anything more elaborate from the Crime Prevention Officer at your local Police Station. The advantage of consulting him – apart from the fact that he has no axe to grind for one particular form of protection – is that he knows what sort of crime is prevalent in your area and what sort of villain is likely to be attracted to your home.

Happily most thieves do not want to break into your home while you are there. So if you can make them think you are home when you are not – then so much the better. This means leaving on all the lights you normally put on during a winter's afternoon. Leaving the hall and lavatory lights on is almost as good as leaving the thief a note that you are out.

Outside lights illuminating your garden and walls are likely to discourage people shinning up drain pipes. You can buy adapters which turn lights on and off in the house at random or time and light sensitive switches which turn off and on at set times or when it gets dark.

In spite of taking all possible precautions you may still be burgled. If you want to help catch the thief or have a chance of getting your goods back, take photographs beforehand of valuable ornaments or jewellery and keep a note of the serial numbers of television sets, radios, hi-fi equipment, cameras and so on. It will also help with your insurance claim.

NOTES

1 *Daily Mail*, 25 May 1977.
2 It is the Inland Revenue Valuation Office or District Valuer probably situated at your Town Hall or local council offices who is responsible for working out rateable values.
3 *How to Pay Less Rates*, Department of Environment, Welsh Office; *Rate Rebates*, Scottish Information Office.
4 Where there are over twenty flats the limit is £25 per flat. There is a free leaflet *Service Charges in Flats*, Department of Environment, Welsh Office.
5 For advice on setting up and running a residents' association, join the Federation of Private Residents' Associations.
6 *Compare Your Home Heating Costs*, Department of Energy.

7 *Warmth Kept In*, Department of Environment; *Control your Heating*, Department of Environment.

8 See leaflet *Money For a Warm Home*, Department of Environment.

9 For addresses see Appendix 3.

10 For addresses see Appendix 3.

11 *Smoke is our Enemy*, Department of Environment.

12 Advice on tackling tricky maintenance jobs can be obtained from Building Research Service publications. For addresses see Appendix 3.

13 National Inspection Council for Electrical Installation Contracting (NICEIC) and Confederation for the Registration of Gas Installers (CORGI).

14 *Bothered by Noise*, Noise Advisory Council; *Land Compensation, Your Rights Explained; No. 5 Insulation against traffic noise*; Department of Environment.

10

Thinking Ahead

This chapter concerns planning for the future while you remain in your present home. It includes improvements and extensions, using your home to get better holidays and where to look for help if you fall on hard times.

Improving or extending your home

Most people make minor adaptations and alterations to their home. But if you live in a house and have the space you might think it worth while extending or altering your home in a more major respect.[1] Alternatively you may have bought a dilapidated house with the express purpose of improving it.[2]

Renovation grants

Renovation grants are available from local councils for the improvement (and sometimes repair) of houses built before 1961. They pay from 50% (and exceptionally up to 90%) of the work done. There are three grants relevant to owner occupiers: intermediate grants, improvement grants and repair grants. With all three there will be certain conditions attached by the Council.[3]

Intermediate grants are given to pay towards the cost of

installing missing standard amenities which are defined as a fixed bath or shower, hand wash basin, kitchen sink, hot and cold water supply to each and an inside wc. If you lack any of these you should be able to get a grant. Intermediate grants must be paid by the local council if you qualify. The grant pays a maximum amount for the installation of each of these standard amenities but can also pay a further amount towards other repairs in order to bring the house up to standard. A disabled person can get a grant towards putting in a second bathroom or wc if the original bathroom or wc is inaccessible because of his disability.

Improvement grants are discretionary and are intended to improve older houses to a good standard – they are not normally available to enlarge a house by adding an extra room. Improvement grants are also available for converting a property into flats. The conditions in respect of the use or state of the property after the improvements have been made will be stricter than with an intermediate grant; you may have to repay some of the grant if you resell within a certain period. Improvement grants are only available for homes with rateable value under £400 in Greater London or under £225 elsewhere. Disabled people can also get improvement grants to adapt their home to their needs.

Repair grants are only available in special areas designated as Housing Action or General Improvement areas.

Listed building grants

If you live in an old building which has been 'listed' as an historic building, you may be able to get a grant to make repairs – and even to carry out maintenance in exceptional circumstances. There are central government historic buildings grants and also local authority grants.

Government grants for repairs are available for buildings of outstanding historic or architectural interest; the grant can be up to 50% of the cost with no upper limit on the amount. There are also conservation grants for the restoration of buildings which are in outstanding conservation areas but do not themselves count as outstanding. These grants are administered by the Historic Buildings Council.[4] Similar grants for use in 'non-outstanding' conservation areas are administered by the Civic Trust which publishes leaflets describing grants in both types of conservation area.[5]

Local authority grants to improve or restore 'historic' buildings vary widely. Loans may also be available from either government or local authorities to pay part of the balance of the cost.

Does your local council approve?

Before you set about extending or enlarging your home you should check whether you require planning permission. Small extensions which increase the size of the house by less than 10% or are less than 1,750 cubic feet, do not, provided that the house has not already been extended by that much since it was built (or since 1948 if the house was built before then). Houses in conservation areas will probably need planning permission for whatever reason and so will a proposed alteration to a listed building wherever it is. If you are in doubt the best way to find out is to call or write to your local council's planning department. Free leaflets are available from them.[6]

There is also a separate procedure for approval under the Building Regulations for England and Wales. For works over £1,000 there is now a scale of charges for this approval. There are different regulations for the Inner London Boroughs and it is the Greater London Council which administers these. Similar laws apply in Scotland and Northern Ireland.

Architects, builders and contractors

The word architect has a specific meaning. It refers to someone qualified as an architect and registered by the Architects Registration Council of the UK. Only people registered by the council may call themselves architects. If someone calls himself an 'architectural consultant' or an 'architectural surveyor', he is unlikely to be registered and may have no qualifications or experience.

Most architects also belong to the Royal Institute of British Architects and Scottish architects also belong to the Royal Incorporation of Architects in Scotland. RIBA operates a centralised service matching prospective clients to architects interested in the type and size of work proposed.

When commissioning an architect the same rules about asking about cost apply as when you are dealing with a new solicitor or surveyor and which are discussed in earlier chapters.

Finding a good builder for an extension can sometimes be a problem. Recommendation is again the most likely route to success. But if not you should provide written specifications for all but the most minor job and get a written contract confirming the terms under which the builder is supplying his services and about the quality of materials used. The advice of an experienced architect can be invaluable in this respect.

It may not necessarily be a good idea to go to a builder recommended by the architect. Should you fall out with the builder it may be that the architect will consider his other dealings with the builder as well as your interests – and he may not therefore get as much out of the builder as you require.

If you are offered a standard contract by an architect or builder it could be worth while getting a solicitor to vet it for you. He may be more persuasive than you in getting unreasonable clauses altered; a solicitor would of course add to the cost so get an estimate from him too.

Another organisation you might approach when considering building work is the National Federation of Master Builders at one of their regional offices in Cambridge, Liverpool, London, Birmingham, Durham, Manchester, Horsham, Cardiff, Bristol or Leeds; in Scotland there is the Scottish National Federation of Building Trades Employees in Glasgow. Telephone numbers and addresses can be obtained from the telephone directory or directory enquiries.

For technical information on repairs and the best way to carry out certain building operations you should contact the

Building Research Advisory Service which publishes a number of very useful leafleats.[7]

Holidays

There are two ways you can use a home for holidays. You can buy a second one as a holiday home or you can exchange homes with someone else for your holiday.

Second homes

At one time country cottages were fashionable and the better off often have cottages and flats abroad in Spain, France and Greece. Sometimes a second home is intended as a retirement home and is bought only a short time before retirement with the intention of selling up the first home upon retirement.

Should you be offered a home with your job – and you already have a home of your own – you could trade in the one you own for a country cottage. This gives you security; should you lose your job you will not have lost out on account of the rise in house prices and meanwhile you will have had the use of it at weekends.

Buying a home abroad is similar to buying one in the UK. But an added problem is the need to carry out the transaction in a foreign language and also the distance from home which may make maintenance more difficult to organise. For many years by law you had to pay the investment currency or dollar premium in order to buy property abroad. This used to work out as adding an extra 30% to 50% to the price. However this was abolished in 1979 and there are now no restrictions on buying property abroad.

Exchanging your home

A more down to earth way of utilising your home for holidays is to arrange to swop it for the duration of your holiday. You go and stay in their home and they come and stay in yours. This can be done within the UK or abroad and can give you the opportunity of budget holidays in places like America or Australia, which you might not otherwise have been able to visit. There are a couple of directories in which you can advertise for a small charge and which contain advertisements from people in other countries who want to make exchanges.[8] This can involve you in quite a lot of work planning and corresponding. But people who have done it swear by it and many do it year after year.

Falling on hard times

Divorced, widowed or separated

If you become divorced, widowed or separated, you are likely to be short of cash especially if you have recently moved into your home. If you have young children things are even worse because you may not have a job. Whilst you cannot stay in your present house because it is too large and expensive, you cannot afford to buy a smaller one because you may not get a new mortgage.

If you are in this position it is essential to get advice. There are a number of pamphlets which may be of some help. In particular the ones published by the Shelter Housing Aid Centre and by the Child Poverty Action Group.[9] These leaflets may also be useful to people who become unemployed[10] or disabled and whose sudden shortage of income turns being a house owner into a very serious problem.

Elderly people

The elderly are another group of homeowners who may have seen better times. By retirement they will generally have paid off the mortgage – and if the main source of income is the state old age pension plus some investments, they will not be eligible for a supplementary pension. In such a case they might consider increasing their income by taking out a Home Income Plan.

The idea is to raise a mortgage which is used to buy an annuity from an insurance company. Generally the same insurance company which gives the annuity also grants the mortgage. By a special tax rule the interest on a Home Income Plan loan is eligible for tax relief in the same way as that on a loan to buy a house. So after all the interest and tax relief and income and tax, the householder gets a net income for life without having to move home. When he or she dies the insurance company is repaid its loan and the rest of the value of the home goes to whoever is chosen in the will of the deceased. Generally speaking you have to be over age seventy for the plan to be worth while; for a couple the youngest must be over age seventy-five. The addresses of companies which operate Home Income Plans are given in the Appendix.[11] An option mortgage version is also available.

Taking in lodgers

If you need to increase you income and have the space in your home, you may consider taking a lodger or letting out a room. The tenancy you create will not be protected by the Rent Act if you change you mind and decide you want to get rid of your tenant (see Appendix 1).

Students are often a good idea if there is a college or university near where you live. The college will often vouch for the students and they will only want to rent the room during term time – and perhaps part of the Easter and winter vacations.

Tax on the additional income may be payable and the consent of your building society to the arrangement may be needed.

NOTES

1 See *Extending Your House*, Consumers' Association.
2 See Ball, R. and Pittaway, A., *The Whole House Omnibus*, Fontana/Collins 1978.
3 See free leaflet *Your Guide to Home Renovation Grants*, Department of Environment, Welsh Office. *Improve Your Home*, Scottish Information Office. *Why Not Improve Your Home?*, Northern Ireland Housing Executive.
4 England, Wales and Scotland each have their own. For addresses see Appendix 3.
5 Grants and Loans available for Conservation, Civic Trust. Conservation Grants for projects in conservation areas other than those accepted as outstanding, Civic Trust.
6 *Planning Permission; Planning Appeals*; Department of Environment and Welsh Office.

7   A list is contained in HMSO Sectional List of Government Publications, *No. 6, 'Building'*.

8   e.g. Home Interchange Ltd.

9   *Rights Guide for Homeowners*, Whately, C. and Tunnard, J., CPAG; *A Woman's Place*, Leevers, M. and Thyme, P., SHAC; *No Father No Home?* Tunnard, J., CPAG 1978. See also free booklet *One-Parent Families Help with Housing*, Department of Environment.

10 For help with the cost of moving if you lose your job see leaflet *Employment Transfer Scheme*, Manpower Services Commission.

11 Save & Prosper Group, Hambro Provident.

11

Moving Out

Having lived in your home for some years you may find you need and can afford a larger one. To find a new home you start all over again with the benefit of the experience you obtained from your first purchase. But one bit of experience you will not have had is trying to sell a house.

Estate agents

Selling a house may be easy or difficult. If it is going to be difficult you will want to use an estate agent; if it is easy you might have a crack at it yourself. The main question you should ask yourself is: Are estate agents worth the cost?

There are no longer any fixed scales of fees charged by an agent and a survey[1] shows wide variation in the charges made by estate agents. This survey reported one lady had paid £480 to an estate agent who found a buyer within twenty-four hours; while another was charged £302 but said it was worth while for having so little trouble. Some of the people in the survey found that they had to pay extra for advertising. And the charges in London and parts of the South-East were generally much higher than in the North; not only was the percentage of the price higher but higher average prices in the South-East also went to boost the estate agent's commission. A bill might range from 1½ to 3% of the price on an averaged size home. In Scotland Scottish solicitors have a scale of commission when acting as agents with a maximum of 1½% (see p. 83).

The golden rule when dealing with an estate agent is to find out exactly what he will charge beforehand, whether this includes VAT and whether you have to pay extra for advertising. Get this in writing from him before you commission him.

Another question to ask oneself is whether to give the house to more than one agent. Quite often an agent will suggest you do not employ another agent but give him a 'sole agency' with or without 'sole selling rights'. A sole agency means that you are obliged to pay him the agreed rate of commission during the period of his agency even if you sell the home through someone else. Sole selling rights means that even if you sell the home yourself you still have to pay his commission.

If you decide to let an agent have a sole agency, and it can be argued that he will try harder if he has one, then you should limit the agency to a specified period of time agreed at the outset. Four to six weeks is the usual time. If he does not get you an offer at your asking price or at a price below it which you agree to accept by then, you are free to try another agent. You can grant a joint sole agency to two agents if you like but this might cost you more. Employing more than two agents can be counter-productive.

Although you have granted a sole agency, the agent may in fact subcontract to other agents. If you really wanted just one agent to deal for you, you may feel cheated; normally however this is only done when the property has been difficult to sell.

It is always best to confirm your instructions in writing, saying the basis on which you want him to be employed. Do not rely on just signing a printed form offered by the agent which is likely to include clauses to your disadvantage. Also be sure your agreement with the agent means that you only pay commission if the deal goes through. If you agree to pay for an introduction of 'someone ready and willing' to buy your home, you may unwittingly have committed yourself to paying the agent commission even if, for whatever reason, the deal does not go through. So in particular make it quite clear that you will not pay if for *any* reason he is not 'instrumental' in selling the property.

What agents do

Estate agents sell property by sending details through the post to would-be customers who have previously approached them. An agent with a prominent high street position or who has a good reputation locally is likely to have a larger list of potential buyers than a new agent tucked away on the second floor who appeals for sellers in the local newspaper.

They almost always put up a For Sale board on the property. They sometimes put details on a card in their shop window – often with a photograph. And they sometimes advertise in the press – usually locally, sometimes nationally for higher priced property; if they propose to advertise make sure you are not liable for the cost as an extra.

An estate agent is also the person to tell you how much to ask for – and whether to accept a lower offer. Sometimes different agents quote widely different prices. An example quoted in the same *Daily Mail* survey was of a five bedroomed house which one agent priced at £37,500, a second at £42,000 and a third at £44,000 'for a quick sale' otherwise £46,000.

People are sometimes suspicious that an agent will buy up their property cheaply and then resell for a quick profit; such an agent is unlikely to be a member of one of the estate agents' associations.[2] It might be best to go to a member of such an association as anyone can call himself an estate agent – there is no formal training or qualification.

However the Estate Agents Act, 1979 proposes that the conduct of estate agents will be regulated by the Office of Fair Trading. The proposals will allow the OFT to ban someone who it considered unfit to practise from engaging in estate agency. There will also be provisions for minimum standards of conduct which the OFT will eventually regulate.

Auctions

If you have an unusual or expensive house to sell you may consider auctioning the property. The auctioneer's fees will be higher than an ordinary agent's but you may get a better price. One problem is that you may find it more difficult to tie up your purchase with your sale.

You can set a reserve price on the minimum you would sell for, and you would be advised to do so. However if the bidding does not reach your reserve, you will have to pay the auctioneer's fee and will not have sold your house.

Selling your home without an agent

Saving money is the main reason for selling your home without the services of an estate agent and if you persevere there is a pretty good chance of success. The first thing to do is to find out what price to ask. One way to do this is to ask a couple of estate agents to call and see how much they say they can get for it; another is to look at similar homes nearby, either in estate agents' windows or in local newspapers, and see what is being asked for them.

The easiest do-it-yourself sales are to relatives or people you already know through home or work contacts. So it is always a good idea to spread around the fact that you want to sell to as many acquaintances as possible. I bought my first house this way from a friend whose agents had failed to sell it.

Next you might look in the 'Property Wanted' column of your local newspaper to see if anyone is looking for property in your area. Where these adverts are from agents they will normally expect you to pay them commission. But if the advertiser is a member of the public then all you pay is the cost of a telephone call to the advertiser.

A more likely way is for you to advertise in the local paper yourself. Do not stint yourself on the size of advertisement you take – a larger one is likely to be more eye catching – and will have space to include all the best features of your property. If you have kept the particulars you were given when you bought the property this might be a basis when you have not a clue where to start. The best way to count the cost of advertising is to compare your total so far with what you would have paid in agents' fees. If an agent quoted you £300 and each advertisement costs £20, remember you have fourteen to go if the first does not bring about a sale.

It is worth knowing that the response to your advertisement can be affected by all manner of events entirely unconnected with your property. These include popular sports events on television, good weather (which can stop people reading the newspapers so thoroughly or at all) or bad economic news, higher interest rates and suggested mortgage famines which deter people moving at all. Do not use a box number and do include telephone numbers attended at all times (home and office) or specify the times if necessary.

You can also make your own For Sale board. This may be worth while as many people tour the district in which they want to buy looking for For Sale boards – a reason why estate agents always suggest them.

In some areas there are property shops or services which display details of your home in a shop or send particulars out on a mailing list. You should regard these as an alternative to advertising in a newspaper and should try to assess whether they are worth using in relation to cost. Estate agents may well respond to your advertisements claiming they have a buyer on their books most anxious to purchase your type of property. Remember you will have to pay their commission if their client buys your home.

Showing people round your home

Whether or not you use an estate agent it will often be left to you to show prospective buyers round your home. Always show it off to best advantage. Make sure it is not cold in winter or too warm in summer. Always have things as tidy as possible and show off any features which are not immediately obvious – like special controls on the central heating or large fitted cupboards.

Once you have done it a few times you will develop a patter, pointing out the view from the room with the best view, talking about the convenient situation for shops and public transport and so on. There is no harm in touching up decorations or giving the place a spring-clean beforehand. Having the house redecorated shortly before you leave may put off as many people as it encourages; they will assume you have covered up some defect – which you may of course have done.

Furniture removers

Having bought your new home and sold your old one, the remaining thing left to do is to arrange to move your furniture from your old to your new home.

As with all the other services described in this book, the same advice applies: get a quote, preferably written, in advance. You can find the names of removal firms in local newspapers, in the Yellow Pages of the telephone directory or by recommendation. Ask two or three to come round: they will want to take a note of what you have in order to work out how much they will charge.

Removal firms generally pack all your china for you, undertake to replace anything they break or compensate you if they cannot. They may be as cheap as hiring a van and trying to do it yourself. Some removers ask to be paid in advance: it would be best to retain payment until the move has been completed to your satisfaction.

If you have a small amount to move and are moving a long distance you might end up paying less if you have your belongings moved as a part load. As with so much else, firms recommended by satisfied customers whom you know are likely to give you the best service.

NOTES

1 *Daily Mail*, 1 February 1978.
2 National Association of Estate Agents; Royal Institution of Chartered Surveyors; Incorporated Society of Valuers and Auctioneers.
3 See also British Association of Removers.

12

Your Home and Tax

An owner-occupier is particularly well treated by the taxman. The tax rules you need to know about are summarised in this chapter. Details change annually and are usually announced in the Spring Budget. For more details you should refer to one of the many tax guides available which have new editions every year.[1] This chapter includes details of the 1981 Budget proposals.

Tax relief on mortgage interest

Mortgage interest is one of the few things nowadays which the taxman allows you to set against your tax bill. And for most people it is completely straightforward. For every £1 of mortgage interest you pay, you do not have to pay tax on £1 of your income. So if your mortgage interest is £500 a year, you can add another £500 to your tax free allowances.

You are allowed tax relief at the highest rate you pay. If you pay tax at 30%, each £1 of mortgage interest actually costs you 70p after tax relief, i.e. £1 − 30p = 70p. But if you pay 40% tax, you are let off 40p on each £1 of mortgage interest and so on. The same applies to the extra tax paid on high investment income called the investment income surcharge. The highest rate of tax in recent years has been 98%. If you paid at this rate your £1 of mortgage interest only cost you 2p!

You should not have any trouble getting tax relief for buying your own home provided it is your only, or main, one. By main, the taxman means a home where you live more than anywhere else.

However you only get full tax relief if the loan is £25,000 or less. If the loan is more, tax relief is available on the interest paid on the first £25,000 of the loan. The £25,000 limit applies to the 1981–82 and earlier tax years. It is possible it may be raised in the 1982 Budget.

If there is a delay before you move in, you get tax relief for the first twelve months – and this period can be extended if there is a good reason. You can also get tax relief if you rent your house out – if you go away for an overseas job for example.

Once you have moved in, you can only get tax relief on an extra loan if it is for permanent home improvements. Decorations and repairs do not count unless they are part of permanent improvement work. Installing a fitted kitchen or central heating are examples of improvements which can count.

Bank overdrafts, credit card and hire purchase debts do not qualify for tax relief whatever you spend your money on. So do not use them if you want tax relief on a home improvement or bridging loan. Get a separate loan account from the bank instead.

Incidentally if you end up in a houseboat or large caravan as your home you can usually get tax relief on your loan to purchase it

For more details see one of the tax guides or ask for the booklet available free of charge from any Tax Inspector's office.[2] See under Inland Revenue in the telephone directory.

Dependent relatives

As well as getting tax relief for buying your own home, you can also get tax relief if you buy one for your divorced or separated wife (or husband), or for a dependent relative. In such cases you can get tax relief on the purchase of two or more homes. But all the loans are added together and must be less than £25,000 in total to qualify for full tax relief.

A dependent relative for this purpose means a relative of the borrower, or the borrower's husband or wife, who is incapacitated from maintaining himself by old age (over sixty-five for a man, over sixty for a woman) or infirmity (receives state invalidity benefit). If the relative is your widowed or separated mother or mother-in-law, she does not have to be either old or infirm.

The dependent relative must not pay rent nor any contribution towards the cost of upkeep of the property. The taxman will ask and you will not get tax relief if the relative does contribute – in however small a way. The dependent relative can pay the rates, however, and this does not count as a contribution.

How to get tax relief

It is one thing knowing you are entitled to tax relief. It may be quite another getting it out of your tax office.

Employed people have tax deducted from their salary and wages through PAYE. How much tax you pay is determined by a blue slip of paper called a Notice of Coding which the taxman sends to you – usually once a year.

When you take out a mortgage, write to your taxman at the address on your Notice of Coding. Tell him how much your mortgage is and the name and address of the building society together with your building society Roll number. Also do not forget to quote the taxman's reference. If you cannot find it, your employer's name and address will do instead.

The taxman will not usually take any action until he hears directly from your building society. This may take a couple of months. So if you want the tax relief quickly and can work out how much it is until the end of the tax year (the next 5 April) ask the taxman to use your estimate until he gets a figure from the building society. At the end of the tax year your building society tells the taxman how much interest you have paid and gives him an estimate for use on your next year's Notice of Coding.

Many PAYE tax offices are out of town. If you cannot call at yours to sort things out, a polite but firm telephone call can work wonders. Reminding letters are often not very effective. Alternatively try one of the Inland Revenue PAYE Enquiry Offices – the wages or accounts department at your job should have the address of the nearest one.

Interest rate changes and tax relief

Tax relief is only available on interest. If you have a repayment mortgage which means paying instalments of part interest and part capital, the amount of tax relief you get depends on how long you have had the mortgage. If the interest rate does not change, the amount of interest in each payment reduces every year – and so does your tax relief.

If the interest rate goes up, however, and you continue to make the same payments, the interest proportion of each of your payments becomes larger – and so does your tax relief. So a rise in the mortgage interest rate can mean a fall in the after tax relief cost of a mortgage. This can work in reverse when mortgage interest rates come down. You could pay more after tax relief as a result.

With mortgage interest rates changing as frequently as they have done in recent years, the tax relief you get on your PAYE Notice of Coding gets out of date pretty fast. There are two things you can do about this. Your strategy depends on whether rates are rising or falling. If they are falling, do nothing. The taxman will do his best to cut down your tax relief in line with falling interest rates. If interest rates are rising, write to the taxman asking him to change the amount of interest on your Notice of Coding. If you can work out an accurate estimate of what the new amount for the whole tax year is, you are more likely to get him to change it quickly. Otherwise he will wait to hear from your building society.

In either case try to check at the end of the year what relief you should have got – and what you actually got. This may be difficult as most building societies will not tell you what interest you paid them in the tax year – only the interest you paid in their accounting year – unless you ask them.

If you are self-employed, you do not have tax deducted from your earnings. You pay it at the end of your accounting year. So you can make sure you get the correct tax relief before you pay any tax.

Capital gains tax

Capital gains tax is a tax which applies to the profit you make when you dispose of an asset for more than you bought it.

Generally speaking owner-occupied homes are exempt from capital gains tax. So is one other home you own where a dependent relative lives rent free. The definition of a dependent relative is the same as when you claim tax relief on mortgage interest for such a home. This is described earlier in this chapter.

If *for any reason* you are away from your home for up to three years but live in the home both before and after, you do not pay capital gains tax even when you rent it out provided you return to your home before you sell it or your then employer requires you under the terms of your employment to work elsewhere.

You can be away for a further four years *provided your employer required you* to live somewhere else. In this case you do not have to move back afterwards.

If you go to work abroad you can be away for an unlimited time and you need not return to the home before selling provided your terms of employment required you to work abroad, or when you come to sell they require you to live elsewhere (in the UK or abroad).

If you have two homes, you can choose which is to be your main residence for capital gains tax purposes. This should be done within two years of your obtaining the second one. If you are required by your employer to live in rented accommodation, nominate the home you own as your main one. Provided you have lived in it for a short while before selling, it will then be free of capital gains tax for up to nine years even if you rent it out – nine not seven years because there is no capital gains tax on the last two years you own a house which has been your main residence.

Also you do not have to worry if you end up with two homes because the sale of your old home falls through. There is no capital gains tax as long as you do not keep both for more than two years.

If you take in lodgers who share accommodation and meals you will not have to pay any capital gains tax on account of them. But if you rent out part of your dwelling separately, you may have to pay capital gains tax on part of the gain when you sell. A new relief proposal in the 1980 Budget allows the first £10,000 of such gains, up to and in addition to the amount of the gain on the portion you occupy yourself, to be tax free too.

The same may apply if you run a business from home. If any part of your home is used exclusively for running a business (you may have indicated this by claiming a proportion of the rates as a business expense) then you will be asked to pay capital gains tax on a proportion of the gain.

This is easily avoided. You claim 'roll over' relief on a business asset (e.g. the part of your home you use as an office) and spend all the proceeds on a similar 'office' in your new home. So long as you keep the business going until you die, or retire at sixty-five, or go abroad and sell after you have left, there is no capital gains tax to pay. This is because there is no capital gains tax on a disposal on death, there are special exemptions on disposal of a business on retirement, and someone resident abroad is not liable to capital gains tax.

Another way round this is to persuade the taxman that you do not use any part of your home exclusively for business use. He may accept this but might not then allow your claim for expenses of maintaining the home which need to be wholly and exclusively incurred for the business to be set against your tax bill.

Extra large gardens – over one acre in size – can lumber you with capital gains tax on the extra size over an acre. And if you are thinking of selling part of your garden, even if it is less than one acre, sell it before you sell the house. If you sell it after you are liable to capital gains tax on that transaction.

I am not telling you how to work out capital gains tax because with an owner-occupied home, you should be able to avoid paying it in ninety-nine out of a hundred cases. For more details of this tax, get the free Inland Revenue booklet.[3]

Capital transfer tax

Capital transfer tax is a tax on gifts and your estate when you die. It does not trouble most people as there is no tax on gifts made between husband and wife during their lifetime or on death.

In addition each partner can give away £50,000 in total to other people in the previous ten years before any tax is payable. Plus £2,000 each in every tax year (which runs from 6 April to the 5 April); £3,000 from 6 April 1981. If you forgot last year you can give £5,000 this year. You can also give £250 each to any number of different people.

This may seem rather irrelevant – you are probably thinking – I need a mortgage and cannot afford to give money away. But someone might like to make a gift to you.

A particularly opportune moment is the occasion of a wedding. Here extra gifts can be made free of capital transfer tax. Parents can give up to £5,000 each. Grandparents and great-grandparents can give up to £2,500 each. And anyone else can give up to £1,000. These gifts must be made (or promised in writing) before the wedding.

So if your parents have offered to help out with the deposit, get it at the time of your wedding and this could save them tax later on.[4]

NOTES

1 For example *Money Which? Tax Saving Guide*, Consumers' Association; *Daily Mail Income Tax Guide*; *Hambro Tax Guide*, MacDonald and Janes.
2 IR11, *Tax Treatment of Interest Paid*, Inland Revenue.
3 CG8, *Capital Gains Tax*, Inland Revenue.
4 See also CTT1, *Capital Transfer Tax*, available from Inland Revenue, Capital Taxes offices only.

13

How to Save Money

Here is a summary of the money saving hints included elsewhere in this book; for easy cross reference use the Index.

1 *Renting from the council:* see if they will sell your home to you at a discount; they may also give you a mortgage.
2 *Renting from a private landlord:* if your home is protected by the Rent Act see whether your landlord will sell it to you at a discount.
3 *Getting married:* money given as a wedding gift can save capital transfer tax for the donor and can be used to make a deposit on a home.
4 *If you cannot afford the deposit:* go to a local authority for a 100% mortgage; try a co-ownership housing association as an alternative to renting; see if you can get into a half rent/half buy scheme run by local authorities or housing associations.
5 *If your deposit is not large enough:* see whether a bank, insurance company or relative will lend you the extra.
6 *If you have a home with your job:* buy a second one of your own now whilst you can afford it and before prices rise.
7 *When offering to buy a house or flat:* do not be afraid to barter

and try to haggle the price down – 5% off is a reasonable figure; make sure extras are included in the price.

8 *When buying a new house:* make sure you have the NHBC inflation linked warranty; the cost is small in relation to any subsequent claim you might have.

9 *Do not buy a mobile home or houseboat:* unless you also have a long lease on a site or mooring.

10 *Ask for estimates from everyone beforehand:* and get more than one from solicitors, surveyors, removers, estate agents, architects, builders, decorators, glaziers, plumbers, electricians or anyone else who does work for you. Find out whether VAT is included (for home improvements there should normally be none).

11 *Do not be put off easily when looking for a mortgage:* be ready to move your savings from one building society to another; do not accept vague refusals; use contacts who can get you a mortgage in place of those who cannot.

12 *Beware of endowment mortgages:* most people are better off without them; only take an endowment mortgage if it is the only way of getting a mortgage – make sure it is with a good value insurance company.

13 *First time buyers:* sign up with the Government Homeloan scheme – it costs you nothing and could qualify you for an extra loan and a grant in two years' time.

14 *Considering becoming self-employed:* move home first; mortgages are difficult to come by for people who have just started up in business or who are not very successful.

15 *Surveys:* ask if the building society surveyor will do a structural survey as well at a reduced fee; if you have a low loan in relation to the price of the home, ask for a reduced building society valuation fee.

16 *Stamp duty:* make sure that what you pay for the home and what you pay for other things, like carpets, is specified separately if their total value is near where the rate of stamp duty increases.

17 *Conveyancing:* ensure that your solicitor is on the building

society panel. If afterwards the fees seem too high, get a Remuneration Certificate from the Law Society.

18 *House insurance:* if your house is unusual, e.g. thatched, make sure the building society has done its homework and the insurance company they have chosen is not overcharging. Check by getting your own quotes.

19 *Contents insurance:* a new-for-old policy will save you disappointment if you make a claim. If you live in London or a large city, check whether you can get better cover more cheaply from another company. Index linked policies are most convenient for all household insurance.

20 *Home improvements:* if your house is in a bad state, see whether you can get help from the local council. Improvements can also make a bank loan qualify for tax relief. Make sure you get a bank loan which allows you to claim it – overdraft, credit card or hire purchase interest does not count.

21 *Rates:* pay by monthly instalments and if your rates are very high do not assume you need a low income to qualify for a rebate.

22 *Disputes:* are best resolved amicably. But if this does not work you would be in a better position with legal expenses insurance to cover your legal costs. Take it out before you get into dispute.

23 *If you fall on hard times:* convert an endowment mortgage to a repayment one, ask if you can extend the repayment term or pay interest only; get a tax relief mortgage converted to an option mortgage if you do not pay tax any more; consider taking in a lodger.

24 *Selling:* have a go at doing it yourself without an estate agent. Make sure you do not sell for too little.

25 *Ending a mortgage:* if there is an alternative to a redemption charge by giving notice, do not forget to give it.

26 *Bridging loans:* make sure your bank does not charge an excessive fee as well as interest. Also make sure a special loan account is opened so that you can claim tax relief.

Appendix 1

Alternatives to Buying

Owning one's home outright is not always an immediate possibility. Here is a summary of the alternatives.

Renting from a council

Council rents are often subsidised and tend to reflect the age, position and locality of a home. The main advantage of a council tenancy is that the rent can be low, the council sees to repairs (although this is often quite slow) and there are no extras to pay. Tenants of modest means are entitled to a Rent Rebate up to a maximum rebate in 1981 of £30 a week (£35 a week in London).

One major problem of renting from a local council is the lack of mobility. It is estimated that nearly a million council tenants in Britain want to move. In theory council tenants can move from one council house or flat to another. But there are practical difficulties in moving although about 200,000 council tenants do manage to move each year.

A delay in a transfer can mean having to turn down a job promotion, or even losing a job if a firm transfers its employees to another part of the country. Growing families need more space – and some tenants just do not like the area where they live.

The main way to move is to swap, which is not a very satisfactory method, as you are unlikely to find people with identical homes in different parts of the country or complementary requirements (e.g. someone wanting more space swapping with someone wanting less) in the same area. A non-profit making organisation which helps council tenants to swap homes is called Locatex – see Appendix 3 for address.

It is proposed to remedy a number of complaints common amongst council house tenants under a Tenants Charter contained in the Housing Act, 1980. This Act will give council tenants the right to take in lodgers and sublet part of their home; they will be able to improve the home and do outside decorations; and they will have to be consulted and be given information about matters concerning them.

They will also be given security of tenure except for a limited number of excluded categories (see list on p. 34). This will mean that a member of the tenant's family living with him or her for six months or more before his or her death will have the right to succeed to the tenancy.

However there will be grounds for eviction even for secure tenants. These include persistent non-payment of rent, nuisance to neighbours, use of the home for illegal purposes, damage or neglect of the home or common parts, or material misrepresentation by the tenant in his application for the tenancy. And in certain circumstances the tenant may be moved to 'suitable alternative accommodation', for example where the council wishes to demolish or rebuild the home, or where the housing was provided for a special purpose as for the disabled.

Security of tenure brings another important advantage and that is the right to buy your home. For more details see Chapter 3.

Council homes are usually allocated by people getting their names on a waiting list and most lists use a system of points – you get more points if you have young children, are ill or disabled, live in overcrowded or unsanitary conditions and so on. These waiting lists are not always as long as they have been in the past but you must usually continue to live within the Council's boundaries to qualify. You can sometimes jump the queue if you are regarded as a 'key' worker – often these are public employees such as district nurses. And if you are prepared to live in older less attractive accommodation, you might find a home, at least temporarily. In London the Greater London Council as well as the London Boroughs rents council homes.

New town development corporations

New town development corporations were set up to organise new towns. Once the town is well established a local council is formed and the housing is passed to the local authority. Tenancies in new towns are very similar to council tenancies although they may be more attractive places to live in and have a less 'municipal' look about them. They may also be easier to obtain than council tenancies because by definition new towns need to attract a new population and they must provide housing otherwise no one will come.[1]

Housing associations

Ordinary housing associations
Housing associations are non-profit making bodies run by voluntary committees of at least seven people. The Tenants Charter (see p. 134) will apply to most housing association tenancies as it does to council tenancies. The right to buy will be extended to the tenancies of some housing associations.

Rents of housing association tenancies can be set by the Rent Officer in the same way as rents for regulated tenants (see p. 139). Housing associations nowadays get a lot of money for new development from local councils and in return the council nominates as high as 50% of the prospective new tenants. In practice they are rather like council tenancies. An official leaflet is available.[2]

Housing associations are often local and vary in size from those with just a few homes to some with several hundred. But they account for about 1% of the total number of homes in the UK.

The Housing Corporation keeps a register of several thousand associations and lends money to them. The National Federation of Housing Associations publishes a directory of housing associations in London.

Co-ownership housing societies

To begin with, groups of architects, solicitors, builders, estate agents and so on with the necessary technical expertise get to-together to plan a scheme. They may not intend to live there – but form the planning committee rather like in an ordinary housing association.

The difference comes about when the co-owners move in. Each pays a nominal fee to become a member of the society and then pays rent based on his share of the mortgage payments which the society is paying. Most societies have option mortgages (a subsidy instead of tax relief – see Chapter 6) so there is no additional tax relief on the mortgage interest. These payments are often called rent and each member has a tenancy agreement outlining his obligations. After the first twelve months if he keeps his part of the bargain, he cannot be evicted.

When a member leaves, arrangements vary. But a typical scheme might return to him what he has contributed to paying off the capital on the mortgage (provided he stays for five years or more) plus a proportion of the rise in the 'co-ownership' value of the property. The co-ownership value is not the same as the market value and depends on how much the new tenant is being asked to pay in rent. People have been disappointed at what they got when they moved.

The sort of people who might find co-ownership worth considering are people retiring or who do not already own their own home and are too old to get a mortgage – they may want a better standard than their private renting or previously had a home with a job. If you do not qualify for a council house or flat and do not like the idea of being responsible for maintenance then co-ownership is a solution.

The disadvantage is that you may find it difficult finding a vacancy as so few are in existence. The Housing Corporation publishes a list of existing co-ownership societies. It also helps people to organise their own self-build housing co-operatives.[3]

Home with the job

If you are a publican, vicar, caretaker, farm worker, game keeper, live-in domestic help or you are in the armed forces, police or fire services you are quite likely to get a home with your job. Generally speaking if you lose your job you lose your home; and if you die your dependents have no right to go on living there. However farmworkers have special protection.[4]

Some employers insist that you live in the tied accommodation so you might not want to consider buying your own home until you need to. Many people who live in such tied accommodation think it is wise to buy their home as soon as they can afford it – even though it may be some time before they will want to occupy it. Meanwhile they can rent it out. There are special provisions in the Rent Act to ensure that you can get the accommodation back when you need it as a retirement home (see p. 138).[5]

Renting from a private landlord

Nowadays private rented accommodation is usually only readily available at astronomical rents suitable for diplomats or visiting businessmen. Anything else which comes on the market is likely to have queues outside the front door in response to a small classified advertisement.

Rents and the security of tenants have been governed by special laws since 1915. They have changed over the years with the result that some existing or 'sitting' tenants have more rights than a new tenant moving in. The result is that 'sitting' tenants have very little incentive ever to move – because nowhere other than in their existing tenancy are they likely to find such good security at such a low rent. But they often suffer from living in a badly maintained building – with a landlord reluctant to carry out repairs as he cannot get the tenant to contribute.

The rules determining the protection available to different sorts of private tenancies are complicated. Most properties come within the scope of the Rent Act if their rateable value was less than or equal to £750 (£1,500 in Greater London) on 1 April 1973.[6]

Private tenants of modest means can apply for Rent Allowances from their local council to pay towards the cost of the rent up to £30 a week in 1981 (£35 a week in London).[7]

Protected tenancies

The protected tenant once he is in occupation has full security of tenure. His landlord can rarely evict him and the rent he is entitled to charge is strictly regulated. Such a tenant is often referred to as a 'sitting tenant' although the phrase 'protected tenant' is the legal term. A 'statutory' tenancy occurs when the period of the original agreement between landlord and tenant runs out or is terminated by the landlord having given 'notice to quit' on a special form. But the landlord cannot enforce his notice and the tenant can continue to live there. If your landlord lives under the same roof see also the section on *restricted contracts* below.

There are a few grounds where a court must grant possession of a statutory tenancy to a landlord. The most important are where the landlord previously lived in the accommodation and wants it back for himself or certain members of his family with whom he lives; or where the landlord bought the home to retire to and let it out before retirement. In either case the landlord must have notified the tenant in writing when he let him move in that he would want it back again for one of these reasons.[8]

If a tenant persistently does not pay the rent, annoys neighbours, sublets the whole home or overcharges a subtenant, a court may give a landlord possession. There is also provision for a landlord to get a court order to move a tenant to 'suitable alternative accommodation' which a sitting tenant might regard as tantamount to eviction.[9]

Sitting tenants are often in a good position to buy their home at less than the market price. Discounts of 20, 30 or even 50%

have been known. Unfortunately many tenants do not take the opportunity and sometimes the landlord is unwilling to sell at what the tenant regards as a realistic price. If the home is in reasonably good repair, an offer from a landlord to sell to a sitting tenant should be considered very seriously. The tenant will be in a strong position to knock down the asking price and he should remember that the next time an offer is made, the price may be much higher.

Regulated tenancies

A regulated tenant is a particular type of protected tenant. Regulated tenancies were created in 1965 and originally only applied to unfurnished accommodation. However since 1974 some furnished accommodation has become regulated and there is now little difference in the rules if you rent furnished or unfurnished.

The rent of a regulated tenancy can be fixed by the Rent Officer, a statutory official who can usually be found at your local council offices. On application of a landlord or tenant, he fixes what he regards as the 'fair rent'. He enters it on the Rent Register and it is then known as a registered rent. The rent once registered lasts for three years after which the landlord can ask for an increase. He can get an increase before this period is up if the rent includes payment for services or rates and the cost of these has gone up. Under the Housing Act 1980 this three year period will be reduced to two. However the rent increase will be phased.

Fair rents are generally a lot less than the rents charged on the open market. Your attitude to the Rent Officer depends on whether you are a landlord or tenant. If either landlord or tenant disagrees with the Rent Officer, he can appeal to a Rent Assessment Committee.[10] In practice the rents tend to be based on what is being registered on comparable properties in the locality.

New regulated tenancies are now difficult to come by, especially in London. If you have one already it could be well worth enquiring whether your landlord is prepared to sell at a discount –

especially if other tenants in a block of flats, say, have already bought.

Controlled tenancies

A controlled tenant is another type of protected tenant and cannot normally be forced to leave his home against his will. Under the Housing Act 1980 it is proposed to convert all controlled tenancies into regulated tenancies.

Restricted contracts

These mainly apply if you started renting on or after 14 August 1974 and you would have a regulated tenancy but for the fact that your flat is part of a house with a resident landlord. If you rented furnished accommodation before that date, you also have a restricted tenancy if you had a resident landlord then. The landlord does not need to share accommodation with you – you both might have self-contained flats in a converted house say. But the building must not be a purpose built block of flats. If you were a regulated or controlled tenant before the landlord moved in, you remain one.

Restricted contracts come under the jurisdiction of the Rent Tribunal which can give tenants limited security of tenure for up to six months at a time. The Housing Act 1980 proposes that for new lettings tenants will no longer be able to apply to the Rent Tribunal for security. The Rent Tribunal can also fix a 'reasonable' rent. This may be the same as a 'fair' rent for a regulated tenancy but could be higher as scarcity of accommodation does not have to be ignored. The Rent Tribunal has its own register of rents.

The main advantage of a restricted contract is that it is one of the few types of privately rented accommodation likely to be on offer. The disadvantage is that security of tenure is only temporary. Such accommodation is likely to be furnished.[11]

Shorthold tenancies

This is a new form of tenancy proposed in the Housing Act 1980 whereby landlords will be able to let at 'fair' rents for fixed terms of between one and five years. The tenant has security for the length of the term but the landlord has the right to regain possession at the end of the term. An existing *protected* or *restricted* tenancy cannot be converted to a shorthold tenancy.

Assured tenancies

Another new form of tenancy proposed under the Housing Act 1980 which only applies to newly built property owned by approved landlords (possibly housing associations connected with building societies).

Assured tenancies will have agreed rents and will be subject to rules laid down in the Landlord and Tenant Act 1954 (which regulates business tenancies). The Rent Acts will not apply to assured tenancies. An assured tenant will have the right to renew his lease in most cases but will have to pay the going market rent.

Unprotected tenancies

If your landlord is the Crown, a Government department or the Duchy of Cornwall the only limit on your rent is the agreement you make with your landlord as is the case of homes with high rateable values.

The same applies if you rent accommodation for a genuine holiday, are a student and rent through your college or university, if you signed a 'licence' to occupy, or if you get meals with your home (worth say 20% of what you pay in rent). It also applies if you share with someone and are not mentioned in the agreement with the landlord, get the home with your job (but it must be a *condition* of your employment), or in the unlikely event of your rent being less than two thirds of the rateable value on 23 March 1965 (unless you are a controlled tenant see above). And if the landlord makes his agreement with a company as tenant, whoever lives in the accommodation does not normally have any rights to have the rent reviewed.

There is no security of tenure in such cases other than that specified in the lease or tenancy agreement. In practice, though, an eviction can be delayed as a Court Order is required for all forms of tenancies even though the Court must grant such an order at the request of the landlord. The advantage of unprotected tenancies is that they may be available. The disadvantage is that they are often at high rents which can be increased without any outside intervention.

If your landlord seeks to evict you against your will you should seek advice from a Housing Aid Centre, Law Centre, Citizens' Advice Bureau or a solicitor at the earliest opportunity.

NOTES

1 See also the pamphlet *Guide to New Town Housing*, Shelter Housing Aid Centre.

2 *Housing Association Tenancies – notes for tenants*, Department of Environment.

3 *Co-ownership, what is it and where*; Self-Build Manual, Housing Corporation.

4 Rent (Agriculture Act), 1976.

5 See *Letting Your Own Home*, Department of Environment.

6 For homes built since then, it is the first rateable value. Homes above these limits may also fall within its scope if the present rateable value is above these limits but a previous rateable value was below former limits. The rules are in the Rent Act, 1977. In Scotland the system is broadly the same but is covered by its own acts. Northern Ireland has a different system of rent control – details can be obtained from the Northern Ireland Housing Executive.

7 For details see the leaflets *There's Money off Rent*, Department of Environment, Welsh Office; *Rent Rebates*, Scottish Information Office.

8 See also the leaflet *Letting Your Own Home*, Department of Environment, Scottish Information Office.

9 See also the leaflets *Landlord and the Law*; *Protection under the Rent Acts*; *Notices to Quit*; Department of Environment, Scottish Information Office.

10 See also the leaflet *Regulated Tenancies: Your Rights and Responsibilities*, Department of Environment, Welsh Office, Scottish Information Office.

11 See also the leaflet *Rooms to Let*, Department of Environment, Scottish Information Office.

Appendix 2

Mortgage Repayment Tables

These tables show the monthly payments you would make to a building society at different rates of interest and over different periods of time. They apply to full repayment mortgages and option mortgages, but in the case of repayment mortgages the cost is reduced by tax relief which you obtain separately from the Inland Revenue; the figures in the tables are before tax relief.

To find out the payments on your mortgage, multiply the figure for your rate of interest and mortgage term by the number of thousands of pounds of your mortgage. For example if you have borrowed £18,000 at an interest rate of 12% over twenty-five years, multiply the figure in the table for a loan of £1,000 by 18. So £10.63 × 18 = £191.34.

These repayment tables are those commonly used by building societies. However you may find that other lenders will quote lower repayments at these rates of interest. This is because they are quoting a true rate as explained on p. 54.

I am grateful to the Nationwide Building Society for supplying the figures from 5 to 16% – the remaining tables were calculated by the author. The figures in the author's tables may be slightly lower than those quoted by a building society.

Monthly repayments of capital and interest on each £1,000 of a building society loan. Interest rates from 5 to 7.9%:

TERM OF YEARS

Rate %	10 £	15 £	20 £	25 £	30 £	35 £
5.0	10.80	8.03	6.69	5.92	5.43	5.09
5.1	10.85	8.09	6.75	5.98	5.49	5.16
5.2	10.90	8.14	6.81	6.04	5.55	5.22
5.25	10.93	8.17	6.83	6.07	5.58	5.26
5.3	10.95	8.20	6.86	6.10	5.61	5.29
5.4	11.01	8.25	6.92	6.16	5.68	5.35
5.5	11.06	8.31	6.92	6.22	5.74	5.42
5.6	11.11	8.36	7.04	6.28	5.80	5.49
5.7	11.17	8.42	7.09	6.34	5.87	5.55
5.75	11.19	8.45	7.12	6.37	5.90	5.59
5.8	11.22	8.47	7.15	6.40	5.93	5.62
5.9	11.27	8.53	7.21	6.46	5.99	5.59
6.0	11.33	8.59	7.27	6.52	6.06	5.75
6.1	11.38	8.64	7.33	6.59	6.12	5.82
6.2	11.43	8.70	7.39	6.65	6.19	5.89
6.25	11.46	8.73	7.42	6.68	6.22	5.92
6.3	11.49	8.75	7.45	6.71	6.25	5.96
6.4	11.54	8.81	7.51	6.77	6.32	6.02
6.5	11.60	8.87	7.57	6.84	6.39	6.09
6.6	11.65	8.92	7.63	6.90	6.45	6.16
6.7	11.71	8.98	7.69	6.96	6.52	6.23
6.75	11.73	9.01	7.72	7.00	6.55	6.27
6.8	11.76	9.04	7.75	7.03	6.59	6.30
6.9	11.82	9.10	7.81	7.09	6.65	6.37
7.0	11.87	9.15	7.87	7.16	6.72	6.44
7.1	11.92	9.21	7.93	7.22	6.79	6.51
7.2	11.98	9.27	7.99	7.29	6.86	6.58
7.25	12.01	9.30	8.02	7.32	6.89	6.62
7.3	12.03	9.33	8.06	7.35	6.92	6.65
7.4	12.09	9.39	8.12	7.42	6.99	6.72
7.5	12.15	9.45	8.18	7.48	7.06	6.80
7.6	12.20	9.50	8.24	7.55	7.13	6.87
7.7	12.26	9.56	8.30	7.61	7.20	6.94
7.75	12.28	9.59	8.34	7.65	7.23	6.97
7.8	12.31	9.62	8.37	7.68	7.27	7.01
7.9	12.37	9.68	8.43	7.74	7.34	7.08

Monthly repayments of capital and interest on each £1,000 of a building society loan. Interest rates from 8 to 10.9%:

TERM OF YEARS

Rate %	10	15	20	25	30	35
	£	£	£	£	£	£
8.0	12.42	9.74	8.49	7.81	7.41	7.16
8.1	12.48	9.80	8.56	7.88	7.48	7.23
8.2	12.54	9.86	8.62	7.95	7.55	7.30
8.25	12.56	9.89	8.65	7.98	7.58	7.34
8.3	12.59	9.92	8.68	8.01	7.62	7.37
8.4	12.65	9.98	8.75	8.08	7.69	7.45
8.5	12.71	10.04	8.81	8.15	7.76	7.52
8.6	12.76	10.10	8.88	8.22	7.83	7.59
8.7	12.82	10.16	8.94	8.28	7.90	7.67
8.75	12.85	10.19	8.97	8.32	7.94	7.71
8.8	12.88	10.22	9.00	8.35	7.97	7.74
8.9	12.93	10.28	9.07	8.42	8.04	7.82
9.0	12.99	10.34	9.13	8.49	8.12	7.89
9.1	13.05	10.40	9.20	8.56	8.19	7.97
9.2	13.10	10.47	9.26	8.63	8.26	8.04
9.25	13.13	10.50	9.30	8.66	8.30	8.08
9.3	13.16	10.53	9.33	8.70	8.33	8.12
9.4	13.22	10.59	9.40	8.77	8.41	8.19
9.5	13.28	10.65	9.46	8.83	8.48	8.27
9.6	13.33	10.71	9.53	8.90	8.55	8.34
9.7	13.39	10.77	9.59	8.97	8.62	8.42
9.75	13.42	10.81	9.63	9.01	8.66	8.46
9.8	13.45	10.84	9.66	9.04	8.70	8.49
9.9	13.51	10.90	9.73	9.12	8.77	8.57
10.0	13.57	10.96	9.79	9.19	8.84	8.65
10.1	13.63	11.02	9.86	9.26	8.92	8.72
10.2	13.68	11.09	9.93	9.33	8.99	8.80
10.25	13.71	11.12	9.96	9.36	9.03	8.84
10.3	13.74	11.15	9.99	9.40	9.07	8.88
10.4	13.80	11.21	10.06	9.47	9.14	8.95
10.5	13.86	11.28	10.13	9.54	9.22	9.03
10.6	13.92	11.34	10.20	9.61	9.29	9.11
10.7	13.98	11.40	10.27	9.68	9.37	9.18
10.75	14.01	11.43	10.30	9.72	9.40	9.22
10.8	14.04	11.47	10.33	9.76	9.44	9.26
10.9	14.10	11.53	10.40	9.83	9.52	9.34

Monthly repayments of capital and interest on each £1,000 of a building society loan. Interest rates from 11 to 13.9%:

TERM OF YEARS

Rate %	10	15 £	20 £	25 £	30 £	35 £
11.0	14.16	11.59	10.47	9.90	9.59	9.42
11.1	14.21	11.66	10.54	9.97	9.67	9.49
11.2	14.27	11.72	10.61	10.04	9.74	9.57
11.25	14.30	11.75	10.64	10.08	9.78	9.61
11.3	14.33	11.79	10.68	10.12	9.82	9.65
11.4	14.39	11.85	10.74	10.19	9.89	9.73
11.5	14.45	11.92	10.81	10.26	9.97	9.81
11.6	14.51	11.98	10.88	10.34	10.04	9.88
11.7	14.57	12.04	10.95	10.41	10.12	9.96
11.75	14.60	12.08	10.99	10.45	10.16	10.00
11.8	14.63	12.11	11.02	10.48	10.20	10.04
11.9	14.69	12.18	11.09	10.56	10.27	10.12
12.0	14.75	12.24	11.16	10.63	10.35	10.20
12.1	14.81	12.31	11.23	10.70	10.43	10.28
12.2	14.87	12.37	11.30	10.78	10.50	10.36
12.25	14.90	12.40	11.34	10.81	10.54	10.40
12.3	14.94	12.44	11.37	10.85	10.58	10.43
12.4	15.00	12.50	11.44	10.93	10.66	10.51
12.5	15.06	12.57	11.51	11.00	10.74	10.59
12.6	15.12	12.63	11.58	11.07	10.81	10.67
12.7	15.18	12.70	11.65	11.15	10.89	10.75
12.75	15.21	12.73	11.69	11.19	10.93	10.79
12.8	15.24	12.77	11.73	11.22	10.97	10.83
12.9	15.30	12.83	11.80	11.30	11.04	10.91
13.0	15.36	12.90	11.87	11.37	11.12	10.99
13.1	15.42	12.97	11.94	11.45	11.20	11.07
13.2	15.49	13.03	12.01	11.52	11.28	11.15
13.25	15.52	13.07	12.05	11.56	11.32	11.19
13.3	15.55	13.10	12.08	11.60	11.36	11.23
13.4	15.61	13.17	12.15	11.67	11.43	11.31
13.5	15.67	13.23	12.23	11.75	11.51	11.39
13.6	15.73	13.30	12.30	11.83	11.59	11.47
13.7	15.79	13.37	12.37	11.90	11.67	11.55
13.75	15.83	13.40	12.41	11.94	11.71	11.59
13.8	15.86	13.44	12.44	11.98	11.75	11.63
13.9	15.92	13.50	12.51	12.05	11.83	11.71

Monthly repayments of capital and interest on each £1,000 of a building society loan. Interest rates from 14 to 16.9%:

TERM OF YEARS

Rate %	10 £	15 £	20 £	25 £	30 £	35 £
14.0	15.98	13.57	12.59	12.13	11.91	11.79
14.1	16.04	13.64	12.66	12.21	11.98	11.87
14.2	16.11	13.71	12.73	12.28	12.06	11.95
14.25	16.14	13.74	12.77	12.32	12.10	11.99
14.3	16.17	13.78	12.81	12.36	12.14	12.03
14.4	16.23	13.84	12.88	12.44	12.22	12.11
14.5	16.29	13.91	12.95	12.51	12.30	12.19
14.6	16.36	13.98	13.02	12.59	12.38	12.28
14.7	16.42	14.05	13.10	12.67	12.46	12.36
14.75	16.45	14.08	13.13	12.70	12.50	12.40
14.8	16.48	14.12	13.17	12.74	12.54	12.44
14.9	16.55	14.19	13.24	12.82	12.62	12.52
15.0	16.61	14.26	13.32	12.90	12.70	12.60
15.1	16.67	14.33	13.39	12.97	12.78	12.68
15.2	16.74	14.39	13.47	13.05	12.86	12.75
15.25	16.77	14.43	13.50	13.09	12.90	12.80
15.3	16.80	14.46	13.54	13.13	12.94	12.84
15.4	16.86	14.56	13.61	13.21	13.02	12.92
15.5	16.93	14.60	13.69	13.28	13.10	13.01
15.6	16.99	14.67	13.76	13.36	13.18	13.09
15.7	17.05	14.74	13.84	13.44	13.26	13.17
15.75	17.09	14.78	13.87	13.48	13.30	13.21
15.8	17.12	14.81	13.91	13.52	13.34	13.25
15.9	17.18	14.88	13.99	15.59	13.42	13.33
16.0	17.25	14.95	14.06	13.67	13.50	13.41
16.1	17.31	15.02	14.13	13.75	13.57	13.49
16.2	17.37	15.09	14.21	13.82	13.65	13.57
16.25	17.40	15.12	14.24	13.86	13.69	13.61
16.3	17.44	15.16	14.28	13.90	13.73	13.65
16.4	17.50	15.23	14.36	13.98	13.81	13.73
16.5	17.56	15.30	14.43	14.06	13.89	13.82
16.6	17.63	15.37	14.51	14.14	13.97	13.90
16.7	17.69	15.44	14.58	14.22	14.05	13.98
16.75	17.73	15.47	14.62	14.26	14.09	14.02
16.8	17.76	15.51	14.66	14.30	14.13	14.06
16.9	17.82	15.58	14.73	14.37	14.22	14.14

Monthly repayments of capital and interest on each £1,000 of a building society loan. Interest rates from 17 to 20%:

TERM OF YEARS

Rate %	10	15	20	25	30	35
	£	£	£	£	£	£
17.0	17.89	15.65	14.81	14.45	14.30	14.23
17.1	17.95	15.72	14.88	14.53	14.38	14.31
17.2	18.02	15.79	14.96	14.61	14.46	14.39
17.25	18.05	15.83	15.00	14.65	14.50	14.43
17.3	18.08	15.87	15.03	14.69	14.54	14.47
17.4	18.15	15.94	15.11	14.77	14.62	14.55
17.5	18.21	16.01	15.19	14.85	14.70	14.64
17.6	18.28	16.08	15.26	14.93	14.78	14.72
17.7	18.35	16.15	15.34	15.01	14.86	14.80
17.75	18.38	16.19	15.38	15.04	14.90	14.84
17.8	18.41	16.22	15.42	15.08	14.94	14.88
17.9	18.48	16.30	15.49	15.16	15.02	14.96
18.0	18.54	16.37	15.57	15.24	15.11	15.05
18.1	18.60	16.44	15.65	15.32	15.19	15.13
18.2	18.68	16.51	15.72	15.40	15.27	15.21
18.25	18.71	16.55	15.76	15.44	15.31	15.25
18.3	18.74	16.58	15.80	15.48	15.35	15.29
18.4	18.81	16.66	15.87	15.56	15.43	15.38
18.5	18.87	16.73	15.95	15.64	15.51	15.46
18.6	18.94	16.80	16.03	15.72	15.59	15.54
18.7	19.01	16.87	16.11	15.80	15.68	15.62
18.75	19.04	16.91	16.14	15.84	15.72	15.66
18.8	19.07	16.95	16.18	15.88	15.76	15.71
18.9	19.14	17.02	16.26	15.96	15.84	15.79
19.0	19.21	17.09	16.34	16.04	15.92	15.87
19.1	19.27	17.16	16.41	16.12	16.00	15.95
19.2	19.34	17.24	16.49	16.20	16.08	16.03
19.25	19.37	17.27	16.53	16.24	16.12	16.08
19.3	19.41	17.31	16.57	16.28	16.17	16.12
19.4	19.47	17.38	16.65	16.36	16.25	16.20
19.5	19.54	17.46	16.72	16.44	16.33	16.28
19.6	19.61	17.53	16.80	16.52	16.41	16.37
19.7	19.68	17.60	16.88	16.60	16.49	16.45
19.75	19.71	17.64	16.92	16.64	16.53	16.49
19.8	19.74	17.68	16.96	16.68	16.57	16.53
19.9	19.81	17.75	17.04	16.76	16.66	16.61
20.0	19.88	17.82	17.11	16.84	16.74	16.70

Monthly repayments of capital and interest on each £1,000 of a building society loan. Interest rates from 20 to 23%:

TERM OF YEARS

Rate %	10	15	20	25	30	35
	£	£	£	£	£	£
20.0	19.88	17.82	17.11	16.84	16.74	16.70
20.1	19.94	17.90	17.19	16.92	16.82	16.78
20.2	20.01	17.97	17.27	17.00	16.90	16.86
20.25	20.05	18.01	17.31	17.05	16.94	16.90
20.3	20.08	18.05	17.35	17.09	16.98	16.94
20.4	20.15	18.12	17.43	17.17	17.07	17.03
20.5	20.22	18.19	17.50	17.25	17.15	17.11
20.6	20.28	18.27	17.58	17.33	17.23	17.19
20.7	20.35	18.34	17.66	17.41	17.31	17.27
20.75	20.39	18.38	17.70	17.45	17.35	17.32
20.8	20.42	18.42	17.74	17.49	17.39	17.36
20.9	20.49	18.49	17.82	17.57	17.48	17.44
21.0	20.56	18.56	17.90	17.65	17.56	17.52
21.1	20.62	18.64	17.97	17.73	17.64	17.61
21.2	20.69	18.71	18.05	17.81	17.72	17.69
21.25	20.73	18.75	18.09	17.85	17.76	17.73
21.3	20.76	18.79	18.13	17.89	17.80	17.77
21.4	20.83	18.86	18.21	17.97	17.89	17.85
21.5	20.90	18.94	18.29	18.06	17.97	17.94
21.6	20.97	19.01	18.37	18.14	18.05	18.02
21.7	21.04	19.22	18.45	18.22	18.13	18.10
21.75	21.07	19.12	18.49	18.26	18.18	18.14
21.8	21.10	19.16	18.55	18.30	18.22	18.19
21.9	21.17	19.24	18.60	18.38	18.30	18.27
22.0	21.24	19.31	18.68	18.46	18.38	18.35
22.1	21.31	19.39	18.76	18.54	18.46	18.43
22.2	21.38	19.46	18.84	18.62	18.55	18.52
22.25	21.41	19.50	18.88	18.67	18.59	18.56
22.3	21.45	19.54	18.92	18.71	18.63	18.60
22.4	21.52	19.61	19.00	18.79	18.71	18.68
22.5	21.59	19.69	19.08	18.87	18.79	18.77
22.6	21.66	19.76	19.16	19.95	18.88	18.85
22.7	21.73	19.84	19.24	19.03	18.96	18.93
22.75	21.76	19.88	19.28	19.07	19.00	18.97
22.8	21.80	19.91	19.32	19.11	19.04	19.01
22.9	21.86	19.99	19.40	19.19	19.12	19.10
23.0	21.93	20.07	19.48	19.28	19.21	19.18

Appendix 3

Useful Addresses

Architectural Association
34–36 Bedford Square, London WCIB 3FS. Tel: 01-636 0974.
Acts as bookshop and adviser for publications on architecture,
home extensions, and how to do it yourself.

Architects Registration Council of the UK
73 Hallam Street, London W1N 6EE. Tel: 01-580 5861.
Keeps a register of people entitled to call themselves architects.
It is their disciplinary body and issues a leaflet containing their
code of conduct for architects.

British Association of Removers
279 Gray's Inn Road, London WC1X 8SY. Tel: 01-837 3088.
Will provide details of members in your area.

British Chemical Dampcourse Association
51 High St, Broom, Bidford-on-Avon, Warwicks. Tel: Bidford-
on-Avon (0789) 772716.
Has a code of practice and will investigate complaints against
members.

British Insurance Association
Aldermary House, Queen Street, London EC4N 1TU. Tel: 01-248 4477.
Publishes free leaflets on different types of insurance including one on how to work out rebuilding costs. A forum for complaints against insurance companies.

British Wood Preserving Association
150 Southampton Row, London WC1B 5AL. Tel: 01-837 8217.
Gives advice on preservation of wood against insects, fire and damp. A list of publications is available on request.

Building Centre
26 Store Street, London WC1E 7BT. Tel: 01-637 9001.
A permanent exhibition of building materials. It also has a bookshop and a library of trade directories and manufacturers' catalogues. There are also Building Centres in Birmingham, Bristol, Cambridge, Coventry, Durham, Glasgow, Liverpool, Manchester, Nottingham, Southampton and Stoke-on-Trent.

Building Research Advisory Service
Building Research Station, Garston, Watford WD2 7JR. Tel: Garston (09 273) 74040.
Advises on tricky design and construction problems by telephone, letter or visit, often free of charge. Has some free leaflets and the Building Research Station publishes a series of advisory leaflets which are available through HMSO bookshops.

Building Societies Association
34 Park Street, London W1Y 4AL. Tel: 01-629 0515.
Supplies list of new members and free leaflet on house purchase.

Child Poverty Action Group
1 Macklin Street, London WC2B 5NH. Tel: 01-242 9149.
Publishes booklets helpful to people who have fallen on hard times. Particularly helpful to homeowners are *Rights Guide for Homeowners* and *No Father No Home?* A price list of publications is available on request.

Civic Trust

17 Carlton House Terrace, London SW1Y 5AW. Tel: 01-930 0914.

Concerned with preserving old buildings etc. Publishes booklets including *Guide to Grants and Loans for Conservation* and *Conservation Grants*. List of publications is available on request.

Consumers' Association

Subscription Department, Caxton Hill, Hertford SG13 7LZ. Tel: 01-839 1222.

Publishers of Which?, Money Which?, Handyman Which? and other magazines. Also publishes a series of books including *The Legal Side of Buying a House* and *Extending Your House* (but as far as building regulations are concerned, the latter is only applicable to England and Wales other than Inner London).

Conveyancing Fraud

27 Occupation Lane, Woolwich, London SE18. Tel: 01-855 2404.

Tells you how to do your own conveyancing. Available through bookshops or directly from author and publisher at the above address.

CORGI

St Martin's House, 140 Tottenham Court Road, London W1P 9LH. Tel: 01-387 9185.

This is the Confederation for the Registration of Gas Installers. You can obtain free leaflets explaining what they do and also addresses of regional offices which hold a register of local installers.

Corporation of Mortgage, Finance and Life Assurance Brokers

88 Victoria Road, Aldershot, Hampshire GU11 1SS. Tel: Aldershot (0252) 315681.

Has a code of conduct and will supply you with names of mortgage brokers in your area.

DAS Legal Expenses Insurance Co. Ltd.
Phoenix House, Redcliffe Hill, Bristol BS1 6FG. Tel: Bristol (272) 290321.
Provides legal expenses insurance. DAS is half owned by Phoenix Assurance and details may also be obtained from Phoenix branch offices.

Environment, Department of
Publications Stores, Building 3, Victoria Road, South Ruislip, HA4 ONZ. Tel: 01-845 7788.
Publishes a number of free leaflets on housing which are usually available at Citizens' Advice Bureaux and local council offices; they may also be obtained direct from the above address. In Scotland the Scottish Information Office, in Wales the Welsh Office and in Northern Ireland the Northern Ireland Housing Executive publish similar leaflets.

Faculty of Architects and Surveyors
15 St Mary Street, Chippenham, Wiltshire. Tel: Chippenham (0249) 55397.
Will supply names of members in your area.

Federation of Master Builders
33 John Street, London WC1N 2BB. Tel: 01-242 7583.
Will supply names of members in your area. There are regional branches in Birmingham, Bristol, Cambridge, Cardiff, Leeds, Newcastle upon Tyne, Sevenoaks and Southport.

Federation of Private Residents' Associations
83 Cambridge Street, London SW1. Tel: 01-834 8921.
Gives advice to individual residents and associations in dealing with problems of maintenance etc., by ground landlords.

Glass and Glazing Federation
6 Mount Row, London W1Y 6DY. Tel: 01-629 8334.
Publishes a number of free leaflets on glass and double glazing. Will supply names of members in your area, who must abide by their code of ethical practice.

Greater London Council
(Housing Loans) TR/H4, 20 Albert Embankment, London SE1
7SS. Tel: 01-633 5084.
Provide details of mortgage loans available from the GLC.

Homesteading Section, The County Hall, London SE1 7PB.
Tel: 01-633 1044/5/6.
Provides leaflet on Homesteading scheme for the first time
buyers to buy up dilapidated property and receive mortgage
without payments for first one to three years.

Hambro Provident Ltd.
7 Old Park Lane, London WIY 3LJ. Tel: 01-499 0031.
Issues home incomes plans whereby elderly people (over 70)
can raise an income from their home without moving out.

Heating and Ventilating Contractors' Association
34 Palace Court, London W2 4JG. Tel: 01-229 2488.
Will supply names of members in your area.

Historic Buildings Council for England
25 Savile Row, London W1X 2BT. Tel: 01-734 6010.
Provides information on repair grants. There are also Historic
Buildings Councils for Scotland and Wales in Edinburgh and
Cardiff.

You will also find the Historic Buildings Bureau at the same
address; this issues a list of historic buildings for sale, including
abandoned railway stations and the like.

HMSO (Her Majesty's Stationery Office)
49 High Holborn, London WC1V 6HB. Tel: 01-928 6977.
The address above is the Government bookshop where you can
obtain all government publications (other than free leaflets). A
free list of publications 'Sectional list No. 61 Building' is available which can be obtained by callers to the above address or at

one of the other government bookshops in Belfast, Birmingham, Bristol, Cardiff, Edinburgh or Manchester. London area mail orders should go to PO Box 569, London SE1 9NH.

Home Interchange Ltd.
8 Hillside, Farningham, Kent DA4 0DD. Tel: Farningham (0322) 864527.
Publishes directory of home exchanges for holidays in UK, North America, Europe, Australasia and elsewhere.

Home Relocation Ltd.
Suite 303, Radnor House, 93 Regent St, London W1R 7TE. Tel: 01-439 3611.
Service by member estate agents to help people looking for homes in areas 'out of town' or some distance from where they live at present.

Housing Corporation
149 Tottenham Court Road, London WIP OBN. Tel: 01-387 9466.
Government financed organisation responsible for housing associations and provides bridging loans for self-build projects. There are regional offices in Cardiff, Croydon, Edinburgh, Exeter, Glasgow, Leeds, Leicester, Liverpool, Manchester, Potters Bar and Wolverhampton. Publications include a list of co-ownership housing associations and a manual on self-build. List of publications on request.

Incorporated Association of Architects and Surveyors
Jubilee House, Billing Brook Road, Weston Favell, Northampton NN3 4NW. Tel: Northampton (0604) 404121.

Incorporated Law Society of Northern Ireland
Royal Courts of Justice (Ulster), Belfast BT1 3JZ. Tel: Belfast (0232) 31614.
The professional bodies for solicitors in Northern Ireland.

Incorporated Society of Valuers and Auctioneers
3 Cadogan Gate, London SW1X OAS. Tel: 01-235 2282.
Members abide by a code of conduct. Publishes a number of free leaflets including *Buying and Selling at Auction*.

Land Registry
Lincoln's Inn Fields, London WC2A 3PH. Tel: 01-405 3488.
Government body which registers property ownership in England and Wales. Check with the head office which of the district land registries in Croydon, Durham, Gloucester, Harrow, Lytham St. Annes, Nottingham, Plymouth, Stevenage, Swansea and Tunbridge Wells, covers your area. Explanatory leaflets on the work of the Land Registry are available from HMSO.

Law Society
113 Chancery Lane, London WC2A 1PL. Tel: 01-242 1222.
The professional body for solicitors in England and Wales. Has free leaflets explaining why it is best to use a solicitor. If you have a complaint against a solicitor, you should make this to the Law Society.

Law Society of Scotland
PO Box 75, 26 Drumsheugh Gardens, Edinburgh EH3 7YR. Tel: 031-226 7411.
The professional body for solicitors in Scotland. Publishes a free leaflet 'Buying or Selling a House' which contains the scale of charges made by Scottish solicitors. Handles complaints about Scottish solicitors.

Locatex
PO Box 1, March, Cambridge PE15 8HJ. Tel: March (03542) 4050.
Arranges exchanges between council house tenants to different areas or size of house.

Money Management
Fundex Ltd., Greystoke Place, Fetter Lane, London EC4A 1ND. Tel: 01-405 6969.
A monthly magazine available on subscription which has regular

surveys on insurance, mortgage terms etc. Single back copies available.

Money Which?
See Consumers' Association.

National Association of Conveyancers
2–4 Chichester Rents, Chancery Lane, London WC2A 1EJ. Tel: 01-549 3636.
Members include cut price conveyancing organisations. Members have to abide by certain rules. Will provide list of members.

National Association of Estate Agents
Harbon House, 21 Jury Street, Warwick CV34 4EH. Tel: Warwick (0926) 496800.
Will supply names of members in your area. Members have to abide by a code of conduct.

National Cavity Insulation Association
178–202 Great Portland Street, London W1N 6AQ. Tel: 01-637 7481.
Members must work to certain minimum standards. Free leaflet and names of members in your area available.

National House Building Council
Chiltern Avenue, Amersham, Bucks. Tel: 01-637 1248 or Amersham (02403) 4477.
Maintains standards for newly built houses and underwrites aftersales service and warranty. Several free leaflets are available. Scotland and Northern Ireland have offices in Edinburgh and Belfast.

National Inspection Council for Electrical Installation Contracting
237 Kennington Lane, London SE11 5QS
Tel: 01-582 7746.
Publishes a list of approved electrical contractors which includes both large and small firms.

National Network of Estate Agents Ltd.
The Cross, Chester, CH1 1NP. Tel: Chester (0244) 42101.
Service by member estate agents to help home buyers.

Northern Ireland Housing Executive
1 College Square East, Belfast BT1 6BQ. Tel: Belfast (0232) 44388.
The body responsible for housing in Northern Ireland; a sort of national local authority. Free leaflets available on home loans and other topics.

Office of Fair Trading
Field House, Breams Buildings, London EC4A 1PR. Tel: 01-242 2858.
A statutory body which looks after consumer interests. It also administers the Consumer Credit Act and will control estate agents. Will deal with or pass on complaints on these and other consumer issues.

Planned Savings
Wootten Publications Ltd., 150 Caledonian Road, London N1 9RD. Tel: 01-278 6854.
A monthly magazine available on subscription which has regular surveys on insurance, mortgage terms etc. Single back copies available.

Royal Incorporation of Architects in Scotland
15 Rutland Square, Edinburgh EH1 2BE. Tel: 031 229 7205.
Professional body for architects in Scotland.

Royal Institute of British Architects
66 Portland Place, London W1N 4AD. Tel: 01-580 5533.
Provides Clients' Advisory Service to help you find an architect suitable for your particular job. Free leaflets available.

Royal Institution of Chartered Surveyors
12 Great George Street, Parliament Square, London SW1P 3AD.
Tel: 01-222 7000.
Association of estate agents, surveyors and building surveyors.
Free leaflets available.

Save & Prosper Group Ltd.
4 Great St Helens, London EC3P 3EP. Tel: 01-554 8899.
Issues home incomes plans whereby elderly people (over 70)
can raise an income from their home without moving out.

SHAC (Shelter Housing Aid Centre)
189A Old Brompton Road, London SW5 OAR. Tel: 01-373
7276.
Gives free advice on housing problems, especially for homeless
and less well off. List of publications available.

Society of Solicitors in the Supreme Courts of Scotland
2 Abercromby Place, Edinburgh EH3 6JZ. Tel: 031-556 4070.
Professional association of solicitors in Scotland.

Index

advance (*see* mortgage)
advertisements
  when buying 22
  when selling 83, 120–1
agents (*see* estate agents)
Alliance Building Society **4**
animals 89, 105
architects 111, 150, 153, 155, 158
auction 27, 120, 156

bank loans
  bridging 51, 53, 59, 85, 132
  mortgages 45, 56, 124, 130
bathrooms 12–16, 23, 103
bedrooms 12–16, 23
board 'For Sale' (*see* sale board)
borrowing (*see* mortgages, bank loans)
boundaries 105
Bradford & Bingley B/S 60
bridging loan (*see* Bank)
builders 18, 104, 112
builders associations 153, 155
building regulations 111
Building Research Advisory Service 113, 151
building societies 2, 45–72, 79, 115, 125, 132 (*see also* mortgages)

building society survey (*see* survey)
Building Societies Association 3, 5, 44, 54, 151
bungalow 15
buying season 11

capital gains tax (*see* tax)
capital transfer tax (*see* tax)
caravans 20, 131
carpenters 104
carpets 23–6, 43–4, 131
cavity wall 102, 157
central heating 23, 25, 89, 98, 102, 103, 121, 154
'chain' (*see* mortgage chain)
chief rent 19
children 23, 24, 105, 106, 151
commuting 8
completion 74–5, 85
condensation 18, 25
conditions of sale 73
contents insurance 94, 100, 132
contract 73–7
converted flats (*see* flats)
conveyancing 73–87, 131
  buying 6, 21, 25–7, 39–44, 59
  do-it-yourself 79, 152
  selling 80
  in Scotland 44, 83–6
  in N. Ireland 86, 155

Conveyancers, National Assoc. of 157
co-ownership 136
councils
  houses 32–8
  miscellaneous 105, 110–11
  mortgages 6, 45, 52, 55
  rates 98–9
  searches 76, 102
  tenancies 1, 6, 34, 130, 133–5
cupboards 23, 24, 103, 121
curtains 23–6, 44

damp 25, 150
deeds 73–87
deposit
  on house 3, 26, 39, 59, 74, 130
  other 21
detached house 13, 14
divorce 12, 114, 116, 124
double glazing 102, 153
dry rot (*see* rot)

elderly 4, 20, 35, 114, 124, 136, 154, 159
electrical 25, 100, 103, 104, 157
endowment mortgage (*see* mortgage)
enquiries before contract 75
estate agent
  buying 21, 26, 68, 74, 79, 83, 98
  do-it-yourself 120, 132
  selling 74, 83, 117–20, 156, 158, 159
estimates 40, 78, 83, 131
exchange of contracts 74, 77
extensions 109–14

fences 73, 76
feu duty 19
first-time buyers 3, 47, 68
fixtures and fittings 6
flats
  conversions 14, 50
  freehold 51, 100
  ground rent 16, 100–1
  leasehold 15, 19, 51, 74
  purpose built 14, 15
  service charge 100–1
  survey of 29

flooding 132
freehold 19, 37, 51, 100
furniture 91, 122
  buying 43–4, 52
  removers 122

garage 23, 24, 98
garden 4, 13–18, 23–6, 51, 73, 90, 128
gas 99–100, 102, 104
gazumping 27
grants
  historic buildings 110–11, 115
  Homeloan scheme 46
  insulation 108
  renovation 37, 109, 115
ground rent 16, 100–1
guarantee or indemnity policy (*see* mortgage)

heating 99, 101–2
historic buildings 110–11, 154, 155
holidays 113, 156
Homeloan scheme 46, 131
Home Income Plans 114
Home Relocation 22, 156
house
  Building Council 18, 157
  different types 12–18
  hunting 8–25
  prices 2–5, 10
  tied to job 1, 35, 113, 137
houseboats 21, 131
housing associations 1, 135, 141
housing estates 20
Housing Corporation 136, 155

improvements (*see* grants)
insulation 102, 105
insurance 88–96, 100, 115
  British Insurance Association 91
  brokers 57, 67
  buildings 77, 89, 132
  contents 94, 100, 132
  legal expenses 95, 106, 132, 154
  Title 82
  see also mortgage
interest rate 2, 47, 54, 60

joint ownership 35, 64, 86

kitchen 13–18, 23–4

land certificate 75
Land Charges Registry 77
Land Registry 41, 52, 74–6, 81, 156
landlords 6, 16, 20, 130, 137, 139
Law Society 41, 44, 77, 82, 131, 157
Law Society of Scotland 83, 156
leasehold 15, 19, 51, 74
legal fees (*see* conveyancing, solicitors)
letting your home 127–8, 133–43
licence to occupy 35, 115
life insurance 52–3, 64–72, 100
listed buildings 110–11
local authority (*see* council)
Locatex 134, 156
loans (*see* bank loan, mortgage)
locks 106–7
lodgers 115

Maintenance 2, 6, 20, 37, 43–4, 51, 77, 101–4, 110
    see also service charges
maisonettes 17, 29
mobile homes (*see* caravans)
mortgage 45–72, 77
    annuity (*see* repayment)
    arrears 2, 114
    bank 45, 56, 124, 130
    brokers 56, 58, 152
    chains 80
    cost 2, 33, 39–44, 64–70
    delay 131
    ending early 70, 132
    endowment 53–8, 61–72, 77, 131, 132
    extending 68, 132
    guaranteed 36
    high start 64
    insurance company 45, 56, 65, 89
    indemnity policy 51
    interest rate 2, 47, 54, 60
    low start 49, 63
    option 60, 62, 67, 132
    100% 55, 60
    payments 2, 53–8, 61–72, 136
    protection policy 64
    registering 74
    repayment 54–8, 61–72
    second 53
    tax relief 6, 55, 62, 67, 114, 123–7
    term 68
    top up 53, 124, 130
    women 47–9
moving house 4, 122

National House-Building Council 18, 131
National Network of Estate Agents 22, 158
Nationwide Building Society 7, 11, 50, 71, 143
neighbours 25, 95, 105
new towns 35, 135
newly built homes 17–18, 50, 81, 131, 157
noise 23, 98, 105
Northern Ireland 55, 63, 86

offers, making 26–8, 84, 130
Office of Fair Trading 60
option 36, 71
option mortgage (*see* mortgage)
ownership
    desire for 1–5
    joint 35, 64, 86

parking 9, 23–4
patio (*see* garden)
pets (*see* animals)
planning permission 111
plumbing 25, 104
privacy 4, 24

rates and rateable value 97–9, 132
Rebate
    rate 99, 132
    rent 6, 133, 138
redecoration (*see* maintenance)
redemption (*see* mortgage, ending early)
registration (*see* Land Registry)
Remuneration Certificate 41, 131

removals 43, 122
renovation grants (*see* grants)
rent charge 19
renting 1, 5–6, 33, 130, 133–42
repairs (*see* maintenance, service charge)
restrictive covenants 19
residents' associations 20, 101, 153
retirement (*see* elderly)
roads 25, 76
roofs 29, 51, 90, 104
rot 151

sale board 22, 119, 121
schools 9, 98
Scotland 10, 21, 36, 44, 73, 78, 83–6
searches (*see* council, Land Registry)
season ticket 100
second homes 113
second mortgages (*see* mortgages)
security 106–7
security of tenure 34, 134
self-build 137
semi-detached 13, 14
service charge 15, 100
settlement (*see* subsidence)
shared ownership 36
Shelter Housing Aid Centre 159
showing house 121
sitting tenants 137–40
sole agency 118
sole selling rights 118
solicitors (*see* conveyancing)
squatters 35
stakeholder 27
stamp duty 34, 42, 43, 74, 131

'subject to contract' 26–7
subsidence 18, 25, 89
survey
  building society 28, 29, 42, 43, 50, 131
  structural 28–30, 42, 43, 77, 131, 155, 159

tax 123–9
  capital gains 2, 127–8
  capital transfer 87, 129
  on rent from lodgers 115
  relief 6, 55, 62, 67, 114, 123–7, 132
telephone 100
television aerials 23
tenancy
  joint ownership 35, 87
  renting 97
  'tied cottage' 1, 35
terraced house 14, 15
thatched roof 89, 132
tied cottage 1, 35, 113, 137
title to property 74, 82
top-up loan (*see* mortgage)
traffic 9
trees 10, 89, 105

unemployed 114

viewing 121

water rates 99
water supply 23, 25
wet rot (*see* rot)
widowed 114, 125
wife's income 47–9
wills 87

DO IT YOURSELF
A BASIC MANUAL

Tony Wilkins

Do you know the difference between a Posidriv and a dowel screw? Do you know how to fix shelves, combat damp, replace a washer? This book will tell you how.

Do-It-Yourself is written for the absolute novice, by an author with over twenty-five years' experience in the DIY field, and is a beginner's guide to basic repairs in the home. It covers such jobs as replacing a plug or a fuse, and painting and wall-papering, often accompanied by explanatory diagrams. Advice is given too on buying materials and dealing with domestic emergencies.

Tony Wilkins is editor of 'Do It Yourself' magazine and has also written the very successful HOUSE REPAIRS in the Teach Yourself series.

TEACH YOURSELF BOOKS

HOUSE REPAIRS

Tony Wilkins

Buying a house is probably the biggest financial outlay you will ever make. However, if this asset is not to become a liability, a continuous programme of repair and maintenance is of great importance. Neglect soon leads to an increasing number of problems and general deteriotation of the fabric.

The problems you meet will, of course, vary according to the type of property you have but, whatever they are, you can make considerable financial savings by dealing with them yourself.

This book will both help you to identify trouble spots and provide you with the knowledge to enable you to do a good job. A summary of the problems you might find, both inside and outside the house, is followed by a reference section of advice on how to tackle them. Topics covered include the roof, doors, windows, walls, damp, house surrounds, floors, ceilings, drainage.

Tony Wilkins is Editor of DIY magazine.

TEACH YOURSELF BOOKS